FRAY JUNÍPERO SERRA

Fray Junípero Serra converting the Indians, woodcut from the original edition of the *Life of Fray Junípero Serra* by Francisco Palóu, 1787.

FRAY JUNÍPERO SERRA
and the California Conquest

by Winifred E. Wise

CHARLES SCRIBNER'S SONS   NEW YORK

ACKNOWLEDGMENTS

Special thanks are extended to the following for permission to quote passages from editions and translations on which they hold the copyright:

Old Mission, Santa Barbara, California: *Life and Times of Fray Junípero Serra*, by Maynard J. Geiger, O.F.M.

Academy of American Franciscan History: *Writings* of Fermín Francisco de Lasuén; *Writings* of Fray Junípero Serra; *Life of Fray Junípero Serra*, by Francisco Palóu.

University of California Press: *Anza's California Expeditions; Fray Juan Crespí*, by Herbert E. Bolton; *Historical, Political and Natural Description of California*, by Pedro Fages.

Academy of Pacific Coast History, University of California: *Diary* and *Narrative* of Miguel Costansó; *Diary* of Gaspar de Portolá.

An occasional sentence has been shortened for clarification. Omission of words is indicated by . . . and of sentences by . . . . Quotations at the head of each chapter are from Serra's *Writings*.

To James O'Bryan Moore,

godfather of this book

CONTENTS

I CALL TO THE INDIES
"Always go forward, and never turn back."

While this is the story of Fray Junípero Serra, founder of the California missions and leader of the first colonization of the west coast, it is also the account of a heroic venture that had far-reaching effects upon the history of the whole United States. Foreign powers other than Spain— notably Russia—were known to be eying this west coast with a view to settlement when, in the eighteenth century, the Spanish king determined to forestall them by sending Franciscan fathers and soldiers up from Mexico. It was Padre Serra's unfailing courage that made a success of this enterprise when the soldiers were discouraged by privation and illness and ready to abandon a project undertaken two thousand miles from civilization.

Instead of a powerful Russia to block American progress to the Pacific coast, the United States in the end had only a weak Mexico to contend with—not the armies of the Czar. Moscow could have ruled the destiny of California instead of Washington.

The Franciscan missions established from San Diego to Carmel and San Francisco among the comparatively docile Indians brought civilization to California. Many times Padre Serra inspired the lonely soldiers and missionaries who came with him to remain through reverses that called for bravery for beyond the call of his duty. Spanish authorities in high places held him in great esteem, and while some who opposed him might call him despotic, the other friars and the Indians found him to be lovable and forgiving, a kind of saint.

Though he had been frail as a child and in later years suffered from a lame leg that made traveling difficult, his mind and his spirit triumphed over his body for the seventy years of his life. He permitted no physical weakness to stop him as he put his soul into work that opened a trail for Americans to follow along the west coast. He was medieval in his asceticism but a bridge into the modern world from old Spain. His zeal had caused him to leave the quiet cloisters of Mallorca for the challenging mission field beyond Mexico City.

Under his farsighted management the California missions prospered and then continued to grow until Mexico had gained its independence from Spain, secularized the missions, and in turn lost California to the United States after the Mexican War settlement. With the discovery of gold and the advent of the forty-niners, the riches the Spaniards had always been seeking became a reality, but Serra had long ago found what he sought—to march with the sword of the spirit.

The purpose of this present narrative is to show history as it happened through the eyes of the men who helped to make it. They have written their accounts in letters, journals, diaries, books—many of them drawn from rare and obscure sources—which have the living quality of personal experience.

One of the most important of these men was Padre Serra's closest friend, Fray Francisco Palóu, who succeeded him temporarily as president of the California missions and who, shortly after he left the side of his beloved companion's deathbed, commenced to write in Spanish a full *Historical Account of the Life and Apostolic Labors of the Venerable Fr. Junípero Serra.* This was published in Mexico in 1787, bound in vellum and closed with leather thongs. Palóu was a fellow Mallorcan who could write with personal knowledge of Serra's days, early and late. Unless otherwise noted, quotations in this and succeeding chapters are from the newest English translation, by Maynard J. Geiger, O.F.M.

> Venerable Father Fray Junípero Serra, that untiring worker in the Lord's vineyard, began his laborious life at one o'clock in the morning, November 24, 1713, in the village of Petra, on the Island of Mallorca. His parents, Antonio Serra and Margarita Ferrer, were humble, honest, and devout farmers who led an exemplary life. As if sensing the great work their newborn son would one day accomplish in baptizing pagans, these devout parents had him baptized

on the very day of his birth. They named him Miguel Joseph. . . .

His devout parents instructed him from childhood in the rudiments of faith and in the holy fear of God. As soon as he began to walk, they encouraged him to frequent the Church and Friary of St. Bernardine, belonging to the Province of Mallorca, in that village. The father of Miguel Joseph was beloved by the religious of the friary, and whenever he brought his young son there, the latter won the affection of everyone. In that friary he studied Latin, learning it perfectly; at the same time he became skillful in plain chant. . . . As a result of these holy exercises and of the devout conversations of his parents, very early in life there took root in his heart fervent desires to wear the holy habit of Our Seraphic Father St. Francis; but to his regret he was still too young to do so.

[Palóu]

VILLAGE BOY

Brown-eyed black-haired Miguel José grew up in a simple two-storied home, like the other stone houses set along the cobbled streets of this farming village in the fertile central plain of the largest island in the Balearics. The overhead loft held cheeses, hams, and the red sausages prized by the Mallorcans, and it was here also that a small store of good crockery was kept and brought down only when guests were to be served. Through the open door to the rear could be seen the mules, which were kept in a small corral so close to the house that it was part of its structure and the animals were practically part of the family.

With its vineyards, year-round flowers, and balmy climate, Mallorca was one of the loveliest of the world's islands and had been a center of Christian culture ever since the thirteenth century, when the Mohammedans were defeated. Windmills and church belfries rose above the olive trees where young Miguel helped his father till their small plot of ground outside the village or went with him to work for richer neighbors. He was a son of the soil, and he was never to forget the knowledge of agriculture he acquired in his boyhood.

Miguel and his father came home out of the burning sun to cool white-washed walls for the meal, which Margarita served them on the plain scrubbed table of boards, and the noonday siesta. They had no luxuries, and the few pieces of furniture were built simply and sturdily for hard years of

3

Geiger photo, Santa Barbara Mission Arch

The Serra house in the village of Petra, Mallorca, Spain.

use. The same could not be said for the health of young Miguel, whose sickliness worried his parents. He was their only son, and three years older than their daughter Juana. Clearly he was not suited to a backbreaking life of labor such as was the common lot in Petra.

Even as a child, Miguel seemed serious beyond his years, with an interest in books that was unusual in a population largely illiterate. It became clear to his parents that if he were to excel as a man it must be through the works of his mind and heart, not of his hands. The bright boy must have a good education, and one of the only ways a poor youth could achieve this in the eighteenth century was to take holy vows.

After long family conferences, it was decided that he must be taken to Palma, which to most of the natives seemed like the end of the world. Content to remain in their villages, most had never traveled more than a few miles from home and had seldom seen the blue of the Mediterranean that surrounded the island. Only a handful of the more adventurous had ever been as far as Palma, some twenty-five miles distant, and returned to tell of the wonders of this seaport city.

Miguel was to go with his father to live among strangers, and Margarita stood in the doorway until the turn of the white dusty road hid them from sight. They would travel on foot, with an occasional lift from some hayrick or cart. Like any mother, she was relieved when her husband returned after many days to tell her that Miguel was safely lodged in the home of a parish priest.

Though Miguel was precocious, sickness had retarded his growth so that his stature was short and slight. Even after he reached the required age, it was difficult for him to convince the Minister Provincial that a swarthy beardless youth who looked to be no more than a child was ready to don the Franciscan habit. Finally he was permitted to become a novice at the age of sixteen years, nine months, and twenty-one days. One of his chief delights in this first year was reading the chronicles of holy men and the story of their deeds and martyrdoms.

BLOOD OF THE MARTYRS

As a result of this devout exercise of reading the lives of the saints, there arose in him a warm desire . . . to imitate them insofar as it was possible. This type of reading caused in him the same effect as was produced in St. Ignatius Loyola. The principal result . . . was a great desire to imitate those saints . . . who had labored for the conversion of souls, especially among the pagans and uncultured peoples. He desired to imitate them even to the point of offering his life and shedding his blood.

[Palóu]

When the year of probation was finished, Miguel José Serra made his profession on September 15, 1731, and took the name of Junípero from that of the quaint lay brother of St. Francis who was called the Lord's Jester. A man of utter simplicity, the original Junípero was so devoted to the poor that he would give away all his food. Taking the vows gave the youthful friar such joy that Fray Palóu recalled he used to say:

"In the novitiate, I was almost always ill and so small of stature that I was unable to reach the lectern, nor could I help my fellow novices in the necessary chores of the novitiate. Therefore, the Father Master of Novices employed me solely in serving Mass daily. However, with my profession I gained health and strength and grew to medium size. I attribute all this to my profession, for which I give infinite thanks to God."

UNIVERSITY PROFESSOR

Serra's height when he was fully grown was not above five feet two, but the brilliance of his mind had already made him outstanding. Even before he was ordained as a priest he had distinguished himself as a student in the great royal monastery of San Francisco, Palma. He had passed an examination that entitled him to become a professor of philosophy, and within five years he had his doctorate in Sacred Theology from Lullian University in Palma. Among his students was blue-eyed Juan Crespí, so gentle and pious that his classmates called him *El Místico* and *El Beato,* who had grown up with Francisco Palóu. Both were to play an important part in the later history of California, but it was the swarthy Palóu who was to become Serra's closest friend and confidant as an outgrowth of these early days in his classroom.

Within the beautiful cloisters of San Francisco, one of the architectural gems of Palma, Serra was becoming known as a man of profound learning and spirituality that steadily increased with the years. He was a constant source of inspiration for the students who sought his counsel. Yet he frequently left his quiet life of study and meditation to preach in the island churches. Here the power of his sermons on morals, delivered in a resonant voice that belied his small stature, made sinners tremble.

> He was preaching the Lenten course [in a village] in the year 1747, and in the midst of the most fervent part of one of his sermons, from among his listeners there stood up a woman possessed. . . . Directing herself in a fit of fury toward the Reverend Father, she angrily cried out in a loud voice . . . "Keep on yelling! Keep on yelling! But you will not finish this Lent!"
>
> [Palóu]

Commenting on this incident with wry humor in a letter to Palóu, Serra wrote that he expected to come through all right and in good health. The devil was not about to strike him down in the pulpit.

He had already gone far in his Order and could expect further advancement and recognition, but he was not fully content. Though he was enjoying the highest esteem and had years of valuable education behind him, he was hearing another call from God that came to him with increasing force. The desires of his youth when he had been fired with zeal to go out as a missionary and convert the pagans had never been entirely forgotten. Now he felt he must act upon them before it was too late. He was nearly thirty-six—an age that for his time was close to old age.

Yet he shared the fighting blood of his fellow Mallorcans, whose ancestors invaded Italy with Hannibal and Britain with Julius Caesar. They were individualists inclined to go to passionate extremes. It was said of them that even when friends met on the streets, they talked as though they were about to exchange blows. Now Serra was stirred to leave the safety and peace of cloistered halls and casting aside all his scholastic honors go forth as the simplest and humblest of missionaries.

Praying and meditating, he planned to keep his inmost wish a secret except from his superior, but a rumor began to circulate through the monastery. It was said that a friar, as yet unnamed, had the urge to go on a mission to the Indies—Mexico, the Philippines, or Peru. This information inspired both Palóu and Fray Rafael Verger with a like purpose. Verger was a professor, but the youthful Palóu could be more readily spared. One day, when Serra was visiting him in his cell, the young man sought his advice.

> When he learned of my intention, he began to shed tears, not of affliction, as I first thought, but of joy. Then he said to me: "I am the one who intends to make this long journey, and I have been sorrowful because I would have no companion. . . . Just now I resolved to speak to you. . . . [since] I was beseeching God to touch someone's heart, it is, without doubt, God's will, since I was most inclined to have Your Reverence go with me. . . . Let us both keep this a secret."
>
> [Palóu]

BOUND FOR THE NEW WORLD

When the two heard of a missionary expedition being recruited for Mexico, they sent their request to Madrid. They were informed that the quota was already filled, but this only increased their desire. Still keeping their application alive, Serra went out to pray with his fellow Mallorcans for relief from the severe drought and epidemics that plagued the island.

He was in Petra preaching during the Lenten season of 1749 when the call finally came for him and Palóu. A previous letter had been intercepted by some unknown hand at the monastery, obviously to avoid the loss of one of the Order's most valued friars. Palóu hastened out from Palma to bear the news to the cherished friend who was ten years his senior; five of the friars scheduled to sail from Cadiz had changed their minds out of fear of the great Atlantic, where untold lives had been lost.

Serra and Palóu could take their places, and at this word Serra's "joy and happiness were greater than if he had received a call to some bishopric." Still, the son of Antonio and Margarita Serra wished to spare them and himself the pain of a face-to-face parting that was likely to be their last. They were both in their seventies, and it was scarcely possible that their gifted son would ever again see either them or the island of Mallorca. Thus he took only another priest into his confidence, one of the same family name. Father Francesh Serra agreed to break the news and give Serra's

8

parents his consolation once their son was well out to sea. Then there could be no turning back.

Back in Palma, Palóu arranged passage on a packet boat to Malaga while Serra preached his last sermon in the same parish church where he had been baptized. Then he hurried back to the monastery for his final farewells and a blessing from the Prelate who had originally taught him philosophy.

> Seeing now the extraordinary vocation of his former student and the great example he was giving, not only to the friary but to the whole province, he [the Prelate] was so touched that his speech failed and he could hardly utter a word. So his farewell was one of tears rather than of words. Naturally the very deeply affected community was touched with emotion at this scene, especially when it saw the Reverend Father Junípero going about at the very last kissing the feet of all the friars even down to the lowest novice.
>
> [Palóu]

The captain of the vessel on which the two sailed was an obstinate "heretic" who insisted upon quarreling with the friars about points of dogma until, bested by Serra, he became so enraged that he threatened to throw both of them into the sea. Palóu warned him that he would have to pay with his head if he did and gave a vivid account of their persecution by the choleric captain.

> One night, infuriated over the dispute . . . the captain placed a dagger at the latter's [Serra's] throat apparently with the intention of taking his life. If this did not take place, it was because God had destined His servant for a more prolonged martyrdom and for the conversion of many souls, as we shall see later. . . . We spent the night awake, in apprehension of what might happen, the ardent zeal of my venerated Father Lector strengthening my weakness and cowardice. But the anger of that perverse heretic was restrained, and during the rest of the journey, he was not so annoying as before.
>
> [Palóu]

After two weeks at sea, they arrived at Malaga, and from there took a coastal ship for Cadiz. Here they were joined by other friars who had been enlisted to be trained for missionary work at the College of San Fernando

9

in Mexico City. Their average age was twenty-seven, and Fray Junípero was second oldest.

Cadiz was one of Europe's busiest ports, crisscrossed with the hazardous traffic between Spain and the New World. For some hundreds of years, it had been the scene of departure for soldiers, fortune hunters, colonists, and missionaries, and for two centuries the harbor for the gold, silver, and spices brought back from the Indies. Often a thousand ships rested at anchor with foreign flags whipping in the wind, and the streets clanged with the activity of a restless and daring age.

"GOOD-BY AND FAREWELL!"

Serra and Palóu were to have a long wait before they could embark, since three vacancies still remained to be filled. When this word reached Palma, three padres moved by Serra's example volunteered and made what haste they could to join him. They were Verger, Crespí, and Guillermo Vicens. On the eve of leaving for his great adventure late in August, Fray Junípero wrote a letter expressive of his deep emotion which is preserved in his *Writings*. It was addressed to Francesh Serra, and it would fall to him to read this to Antonio and Margarita, as they were illiterate.

> Dear intimate friend: Words cannot express the feelings of my heart as I bid you farewell nor can I properly repeat to you my request that you be the consolation of my parents to sustain them in their sorrow. I wish I could communicate to them the great joy that fills my heart. If I could do this, then surely they would always encourage me to go forward and never turn back. . . .
>
> Since they are advanced in years, let them recall that life is uncertain and, in fact, may be very brief. If they compare it with eternity, they will clearly realize that it cannot be more than an instant. . . .
>
> Tell them that I shall ever feel the loss of not being able to be near them and therefore to console them, but since first things must come first and before all else, the first thing to do is to fulfill the will of God. It was for the love of God that I left them. . . .
>
> Let them rejoice that they have a son who is a priest, though an unworthy one and a sinner, who daily in the holy sacrifice of the Mass prays for them with all the fervor in his soul. . . .

Good-by, my dear father! Farewell, dear mother of mine! Good-by, my dear sister Juana! Good-by, my beloved brother-in-law. Take good care of Miquelet and see to it that he becomes a good Christian and a studious pupil and that the two girls grow up as good Christians. Trust to God that your uncle may yet be of some service to you. Good-by and farewell!

II   NEW SPAIN

"If I were continually to keep before my mind what I had left behind, what use would it be to leave at all?"

Serra sealed the letter, which also bore specific mention of all his fondest friends in Petra, and crossed the gangplank of a small ship that was in poor condition to meet the battering of the Atlantic. Because of the delay in departure, it would be running into severe equinoctial storms, tossed like a hogshead among the waves. The ship was to make bad sailing time, but Serra, unlike his companions, was never seasick. Palóu recorded his friend's behavior on the perilous journey.

On the long voyage of ninety-nine days which it took to reach Veracruz, many inconveniences and scares befell us. For in the reduced space of the ship it was necessary to accommodate, besides our mission band [of twenty-two], another composed of Reverend Dominican Fathers [seven], and many passengers of note. Because of the scarcity of water which we experienced during the fifteen days preceding our arrival at Puerto Rico, we were rationed to such an extent that the amount they gave us each twenty-four hours was hardly more than a pint, so that it was impossible even to make chocolate. But Fray Junípero suffered these inconveniences with such patience that he was never heard to utter the least complaint. . . His companions . . . were wont to ask him if he were not thirsty. To this he answered: "It is nothing to worry about." And if anyone complained that he could not stand the thirst, he would answer . . . "I have found a means to avoid thirst, and it is this: to eat little and talk less in order not to waste the saliva."

The missionaries disembarked in San Juan without a coin among them, but the people were so hospitable that, as Serra wrote back to Petra, they "ate and drank better than in any monastery, even chocolate, pipe tobacco and snuff and lemonade in the afternoon being served to one's fancy." While here they conducted a Mission and preached to great throngs. The enthusiasm was such that for days they had to stay in the confessionals "beginning as early as three or four o'clock in the morning, and in the afternoons, too, and we did not finish until midnight."

NEAR SHIPWRECK

Outside of Puerto Rico, they went aground upon rocks that caused serious damage, but the ship floated free with the tide to continue on toward Veracruz. They were not far distant from this port when a violent storm threatened to wreck the crippled ship.

> There arose a hurricane so violent that we were obliged to head toward the Sound of Campeche. On the way thither we ran into such a violent storm lasting through December 3 and 4, that during the night of the 4th we gave ourselves up for lost. We had no other recourse than to prepare ourselves for death. But our Fray Junípero, in the midst of that great storm, retained as undisturbed a peace and as tranquil a mind as if he were experiencing the most serene day.
>
> When he was asked if he were afraid, he answered: "A little." But when he remembered the purpose for which he had come to the Indies, even this fear left him immediately. His tranquillity remained unchanged when during the night we learned that the ship's crew had mutinied against the captain and the pilots, asking that the ship be run ashore so that some at least could be saved. Neither could the vessel bear the tempest nor could the pumps expel the water it was shipping.
>
> [Palóu]

In this desperate moment, the various friars each wrote the name of his favorite saint on a piece of paper, which he tossed into a bowl. When they drew lots, the choice fell to St. Barbara, and they implored her intervention.

All cried loudly: "Long live St. Barbara!" In that instant the tempest ceased and the adverse wind became so mild that within the next two days, on December 6, we arrived at Veracruz.

[Palóu]

The mainmast was gone, and the ship was filled with gaping holes. Inspection showed that one more day of storm would have sent them all to the bottom.

250 MILES ON FOOT

Once arrived in Veracruz, their party was urged to hasten its course to the higher altitudes of Mexico City. Swamps surrounded the seaport, making it a breeding ground for yellow fever and malaria, and Palóu became so ill before they could depart that he came close to death. They had a hundred-league journey ahead of them with transportation on horseback furnished at royal expense. Because of the long sea voyage and the sudden changes in climate here in Mexico, it was felt they must have this comfort, but Serra refused it. He wished to follow the example of St. Francis and walk the whole distance of around two hundred and fifty miles along the old circuitous route of *El Camino Real* (The King's Highway). Accompanied by another gray-robed friar of equal zeal, he set out with only his breviary and Providence as a guide through hostile deserts, tropical jungles, and high mountains.

It was night when they reached the banks of a river that lay between them and the next village. Its swollen waters made it folly to attempt to cross unless they found the ford. After saying a prayer, they thought they saw a dim form moving on the opposite shore. Serra called out, and a man answered with the offer to act as their guide. Once they were safely across, he took them to his house and fed and sheltered them through a night so wintry that the road was covered with ice. Without his timely aid, they would have perished.

Again along the route, when they were exhausted by the heat of the day and the steepness of their climb, a man appeared suddenly to offer them each a pomegranate, which sustained them until they could reach the next hacienda. On another occasion, they had only a loaf of bread which they gave to a beggar who asked for alms. They were a long way from the inn where they hoped to spend the night, and finally they sat

A portion of *El Camino Real.*

beside the road, too footsore and famished to walk another mile. A man on horseback reared to a stop, and breaking a loaf of corn bread in half, offered a portion to each of the padres. It was an unaccustomed food and appeared to be only half-baked, so that they were afraid to eat it until hunger gave them no choice. They found it delicious, and another example of being sustained by their faith.

At various times, the Venerable Father Junípero mentioned these events in order to exhort his hearers to trust in divine Providence.

He said that the benefactor was either the Patriarch St. Joseph or some devout man whose heart this Saint touched to do these acts of charity toward them.

[Palóu]

The journey on foot, in sandals, of fifteen and twenty miles a day was to have its consequences also in the bite of a mosquito, possibly the vicious *zancudo,* which sent Padre Serra hobbling along the road and finally made him take rest on a farm. He had scratched the leg during his sleep until it became infected and caused an ulcer that was never entirely to disappear. At times during the rest of his life, it would flare up to cause him agony.

Their destination was the College of San Fernando, one of the centers for the training of missionaries. Serra was to become one of the most illustrious ever to enter the mission field, and he arrived at the College on the first of the new year. Mexico City was a place of splendor and squalor with nearly a hundred thousand inhabitants, half of them white and half of mixed blood. Bazaars were rich with the treasure of the Indies brought to them by the Manila galleons—silks and brocades and porcelains from the Far East. Luxurious carriages rolled along wide streets lined with beggars and heaps of refuse. It was a city of great social contrast.

In the two centuries and more since Cortés had conquered Mexico and overthrown the astounding civilization of the Aztecs, great cathedrals had risen as testimony to the triumph of New Spain. The faithful worshiped before magnificent altars laden with candlesticks and sacred vessels of solid silver and gold, but the ancient gods still held their grip in the mountains that were remote from wealthy populous centers such as Guadalajara and Mexico City. By Fray Junípero's time, some four thousand missionaries were trying to change the native beliefs in the New World colonies of Spain, the first of them having arrived with Columbus. Now more were needed to push on from older provinces to distant frontiers.

At the College, Serra asked to be allowed to go through a refresher period in order to "revive in his heart those desires which he had felt as a novice, which had been deadened somewhat by the distraction of his studies." Serving as a novice once more would "light in his heart the love for his fellow men" and "give birth in him the most vivid desire to shed his blood, if necessary, in order to secure the salvation of the miserable gentiles." [Palóu]

Noting Serra's extreme fervor and dedication, one of the aged founders of the College embraced him with the remark, "Would that someone would bring us a forest of junipers." [Palóu]

"HERE AM I. SEND ME"

It was June before he was ready to be sent into the field and, with Palóu, departed for the Sierra Gorda. This was a region so hot and humid that several friars had died there trying to convert the Pame Indians. They had long preferred to roam the mountains than to be civilized by the missions, and Serra was to spend the next nine years among them.

Many at the College deplored the waste of a man of his intellectual stature and force in such a pursuit, but he had been first to volunteer when the call came. He had had his fill of prestige, and it was as a simple missionary that he planned to spend the rest of his life. Using the words of Isaiah, he had said in Latin, "Here am I. Send me."

Traveling again on foot, though pack animals were offered and his leg was still painful, Serra and his companion made the long hard journey to the Mission of Santiago de Xalpan. Here the university professor was to learn the rudiments of the mission field as enthusiastically as a bright child might learn his ABC's. From the first, he had a great love of the Indians which was translated into many forms.

> Seeing these missions in so backward a state . . . he applied himself immediately to learning their language. For this purpose he had as teacher an Indian from Mexico City who had been reared among the Pames. . . . Thus he began to pray with the Indians in their native tongue, every other day alternating it with the catechism in Spanish. In this way the Indians were instructed in the mysteries of our Holy Faith in a very short time.
>
> [Palóu]

He was quick to see also that these people could not understand the abstractions of doctrine, but that it must be presented to them with all the splendor and drama that he could devise. He sent to Mexico City for a lovely statue of the Virgin "which was put on a platform and taken out in procession through the town every Saturday night, the illumination being made with lanterns, and with the accompaniment of the Rosary." The children were taught to present a nativity play at Christmas time, and "during the Lenten season he did not spare himself in his devotion to his desire to move the hearts of the neophytes." He ordered the Chapel of Calvary built on a hill outside the town and on Fridays led a procession there carrying a cross that, as Palóu wrote, "was so heavy that I, who was younger and stronger than he, could scarcely lift it."

Church of Santiago de Xalpan.

Geiger photo, Santa Barbara Mission Arc

On Holy Thursday, after having washed the feet of twelve of the oldest Indians and eaten with them, he preached the sermon. . . At night he held a procession with the image of the Christ Crucified in which the whole town participated. On Friday morning he preached a sermon on the Passion, and in the afternoon, in the most realistic manner, the Descent from the Cross was represented. This was done by means of a lifelike image which was ordered with hinges made for that purpose. . . .

By means of such devout exercises he could not but instill in the neophytes a great and tender devotion. Because of it, they prepared themselves to celebrate Holy Week each year. The news also spread to the neighboring towns inhabited by Spaniards, and these likewise came to celebrate it, attracted by the report of the devotion of the Indians.

[Palóu]

Yet hungry Indians did not make good converts, and they must be fed lest they go back to the mountains. They must be taught how to work, and the fields must be cultivated along with their souls. Here Serra revealed the practical side of his nature and the gift for organization that was to make him one of the greatest and most successful of missionaries. He had been raised on the soil. Mindful of the admonition from his superiors that the Indians must have what they needed to eat and wear, he advanced the Xalpan neighborhood to a new degree of prosperity and civilization.

To bring this about he obtained . . . bulls, cows, and other animals such as pigs and sheep; and maize and beans in order to plant a crop immediately. . . . By this means he in a short time obtained some kind of harvest, which increased year by year. This was distributed daily after the recitation of the Christian doctrine. When . . . these harvests increased and became so abundant that there was some left over and above the needs of sustenance, he instructed the Indians to sell the remainder . . . under the direction of the fathers. With this money more yoke of oxen were bought, while the tools and other necessary articles for work were increased. . . . He always presented the tillers with a special gift [of blankets or cloth] to reward them . . .

and to attract the rest to this form of labor, which is the most difficult and also the most necessary.

[Palóu]

Like a father at the head of a large family, Serra was weaning the Indians
away from what he considered to be idleness and improvidence. He and
Palóu watched to see that they were not cheated in their innocence of
matters of trade and encouraged the women to sell their wares. Trained
masons, carpenters and blacksmiths came to teach the Indian men, while
the women and children engaged in the arts of spinning, weaving, and
sewing.

His work drew upon all his skills, but within a few years he was able
to start the building of a large stone church to replace an old thatched
adobe that was in miserable shape and could not hold all the converts.
Serra himself often worked on it as a common laborer along with the
Indians until at the end of seven years it was finally completed with the
exquisite carved façade that still makes it a choice example of the Spanish
Colonial style.

> He also joined in with the masons to fill the crevices between the
> stones with rubble to strengthen the walls. All this he did in the
> most humble sort of clothing, wearing a habit that had become tat-
> tered, wrapping around himself a piece of an old mantle, despite the
> fact that the land is very hot. For sandals he wore a piece of crude
> leather, the footgear of those Indians. . . . [A visitor from the College
> was taken aback.] He saw him one day among a group of Indians,
> more than twenty in number, who were carrying a large beam, and
> he was helping them carry it. Since he was shorter than the others,
> he inserted a piece of his mantle between his shoulder and the beam
> to equalize it. . . . And he [the visitor] said to me: "Look at your pro-
> fessor, and see how he is making the Way of the Cross, and in what
> garments!" But I answered him: "This happens every day."

[Palóu]

Serra's abilities were not long in being recognized; he had made himself
so outstanding that he could no longer decline the executive post of
President of all five Sierra Gorda missions. He was frequently on the road

between them, and it was not until 1758 that he was recalled to Mexico City.

> He left his Indians well instructed, as before described. With him he carried, as a trophy of the victorious triumph he had obtained over Hell, the chief idol which those unhappy Indians had formerly adored as their god. This idol was a perfectly formed face of a woman, made of white transparent marble. . . They had placed this on the highest point of an elevated mountain range, within a house fashioned like an idol-temple. . . . . The native name which the Indians gave to that idol was Cachum, which means Mother of the Sun. . . . An aged Indian was custodian of the idol. He performed the office as minister of the demon.
>
> [Palóu]

FERVENT FRIAR

Where many another missionary had been tested in the arduous field and failed or even gone back to Spain, Fray Junípero had fully proved his endurance, his strength, and his insight into the hearts of native peoples. Now he was being called upon to undertake the spiritual conquest of the Apaches in what is now Texas. One padre had recently been killed there, and another was recuperating from his wounds, but Serra's face was radiant with a new "joy and happiness." It was an expedition that had to be delayed until the San Saba region was again a safe place in which to live; and it never took place.

> This turn of events was a source of deep sorrow to the zealous Father Junípero. But he did not lose merit before God for having voluntarily offered himself for such a difficult enterprise, with the evident danger of dying at the hands of those barbarous and cruel pagans.
>
> [Palóu]

Instead, Fray Junípero made his headquarters in Mexico City, preaching his fervent sermons in the capital or going out to various towns to redeem the sinners, often with graphic demonstrations.

Not content to mortify his body for his own imperfections and sins, he also did penance for the sins of others. By strong censures he would move his listeners to sorrow and penance for their sins. He struck his breast with a stone, in imitation of St. Jerome. In imitation of St. Francis Solanus, to whom he was devoted, he used the chain to scourge himself. He used the burning torch, applying it to his uncovered chest, burning his flesh in imitation of St. John Capistran and various other saints. All this he did with the purpose not only of punishing himself, but also of moving his hearers to penance for their own sins.

[Palóu]

On one such occasion, a man in the congregation leaped forward to take the chain from Serra and, in repentance, beat himself so violently that he collapsed. After receiving the Last Sacraments, he died.

There were many who were targets of Serra's anger. Leading an austere life himself, Serra did not spare the wealthy women of Mexico City. For them, churchgoing was apt to be a social occasion at which servants served them cups of chocolate. They sat unmoved while he railed at them for their indolence and hypocrisy, waiting only for the service to end so that they could go into the courtyard to gossip.

He also aroused secret enemies with his fiery sermons. One day it appeared that the sacramental wine had been poisoned, but he refused to show fear.

While the servant of God was celebrating Mass, it seemed to him that when he was consuming the Precious Blood he had imbibed a heavy weight as if it were lead, so that he visibly changed color and was rendered partly speechless. Nevertheless, he took the second ablution, but as soon as he consumed it he lost his speech altogether. If it had not been for the fact that one of those attending Mass was quickly at hand, the Venerable Father would have fallen to the floor.

[Palóu]

He was carried into the sacristy and placed on a bed where he was given a cup of oil. All believed that someone had put poison in the wine cruet in order to kill him. Shortly he felt better, and the first words he spoke were those from St. Mark: "If they drink any deadly thing, it shall not hurt them."

In order to reach the capital of Oaxaca . . . [he] had to sail for eight days along the large Los Miges River. During this journey both he and his companions were forced to suffer many hardships by reason of the excessive heat, molestation from mosquitoes, the threat of alligators. Nor were they able to leave their canoe to go on land because of the tigers and lions [jaguars and pumas], serpents and other poisonous animals with which those regions abound (for which reason they are uninhabited by humans).

[Palóu]

At times his experiences bordered on the miraculous, as when he was traveling a lonely road from Huasteca with his companions.

One day during the journey, when the sun had already set, the missionaries did not know where to go for a night's lodging, believing for certain that they would have to spend the night in the open fields . . . when they saw a house a short distance away, close to the highway. Within they found a venerable man with his wife and a child, who graciously offered them shelter. With unusual neatness and kindness, they also served them supper.

After the fathers had said farewell next morning . . . they continued their journey. At a short distance they met some muleteers, who asked them where they had spent the night. The missionaries replied they stayed in the house near the road. "Which house?" queried the muleteers. "Along the entire road you traveled yesterday, there was not a house or a ranch for many leagues." The fathers stood looking at one another in wonderment, while the muleteers repeated their statement that there was no such house along the road. The missionaries then believed that it had been divine Providence which had granted them the favor of that hospitality, and that undoubtedly those persons who were within the house were Jesus, Mary, and Joseph.

[Palóu]

23

During the years from 1758 to 1767, Fray Junípero walked over five thousand miles despite his lame leg. He was a singular man, a complex individual of enormous drive. Subduing his human passions with penance and self-castigation, he channeled his energies into the conversion of sinners and the saving of souls. Many sought him out as their father confessor, and he was a salient figure in Mexico City, which with all its monasteries, convents, and churches had almost become another Rome.

> He was serious from childhood, which seriousness he retained all through his life, so that exteriorly he appeared to be austere and almost unapproachable. But as soon as one talked and dealt with him, one had to change his opinion and consider him gentle, amiable, and attractive, for he won the hearts of all. At the same time, he was bashful, particularly with those he had not met before. When he was in the presence of women, he always was serious and modest, both in his glances and in his speech, endeavoring to turn the conversation to holy and edifying topics, recounting some events and acts from the lives of the saints.
>
> [Palóu]

When the Jesuits were expelled from the Lower California missions in 1767—as a result of distrust in the Spanish court over the Order's growing wealth and power in Europe—the Franciscans were asked to replace them. If anyone could make the mission system prosper in this poor, bleak, remote peninsula, it would be Fray Junípero Serra. He was the natural choice for President.

The mission system was Spain's answer to the problem of colonization and a spreading of the culture and influence of a small nation over more than half of two American continents. More humanitarian than other methods, it aimed to adapt the native Indian to civilization where the English drove him back, and backwoods settlers took the stand that the only good Indian was a dead one. The French pioneer was the fur trader and the missionary; the Spanish pioneer was the soldier sent out with the missionary to hold frontier outposts as nuclei of expansion and defense.

The Spanish missionary was a prime agent of both Church and State, expected to win the friendship and trust of the aborigines and create centers where they could be converted to Christianity and educated to useful labor. Lacking Spanish colonists in any great numbers, the government had come to look to the missionary to give vitality to the whole system. If he failed in any region, the failure was apt to be total.

Again Fray Junípero traveled along *El Camino Real,* this time six hundred miles to the Pacific Ocean. With him were his old friends Crespí and Palóu. Among the other Franciscans was a third padre whose name would prove to be highly significant—that of Fermín Francisco de Lasuén. They had been told to expect little of Lower California, where converts had been few and the pearls and gold presumably accumulated by the Jesuits a myth. The missions there were straggling, but it was rumored that the government had further plans for the brilliant padre who headed the expedition.

III   "FOR THE GLORY OF GOD"

"Where will the ox go which does not fare forth to the plough, but to the block?"

The high government of Spain being informed of the repeated attempts of a foreign nation upon the northern coasts of California, with designs by no means friendly to the monarchy and its interests, the king [Carlos III] gave orders to the Marquis de Croix, his Viceroy and captain-general of New Spain, that he should take effective measures to guard that part of his dominions from all invasion and insult.

Thus wrote Don Miguel Costansó, who was army engineer and cosmographer of the expedition, of which Fray Junípero was the spiritual leader, that in 1769 was sent to settle Upper California. Costansó was a man of high intelligence and acute observation. His *Narrative* of the journey was printed originally in 1770 and immediately suppressed by the Spanish government. The reason doubtless was to keep the information it contained from falling into the hands of "a foreign nation," for Costansó clearly exposed the weakness of Spain. The power of chief concern was Russia, whose growing friendliness with England, Spain's traditional enemy, made it a double threat since England had recently won against the French in North America and might decide to advance westward.

Though Spanish officials might insist that the chief object was to convert the pagans of Upper California to Christianity, they also had another stake in this game of international politics. Russian fur traders were pushing down from Alaska, and the dust of centuries had gathered on the old charts made by earlier Spanish explorers.

Juan Rodríguez Cabrillo had discovered Upper California in 1542 while seeking treasure and the Strait of Anían, mythical passage to the Orient. He sailed his ship into San Diego Bay, and in 1602 Sebastián Vizcaíno had found the bay of Monterey. Now the time had come when Spain's claim to the region must be re-established by active settlement. The land must be held in practice, as well as theory, by the system which Spain had found workable elsewhere. This was to set up a chain of missions to civilize the native Indians and serve as an attraction to immigrants from Mexico. The calculations were not lost upon Costansó, whose chronicle follows as a valuable record.

The Marquis de Croix had facilitated the plans of the king in this matter [of securing both the Californias] inasmuch as, previous to receiving this order, he had, at the time of the expulsion of the Jesuits from New Spain, appointed a political and military governor of [Lower] California to carry out the operation of that province, to keep it in obedience to the king, preserve it in peace, and give information of any event that might occur.

His Excellency had also resolved to send to the peninsula [of Lower California] men of intelligence, employed exclusively to explore and examine the known parts of it. . . . At this juncture, Don José de Gálvez . . . removed the weight of this difficulty by offering to go in person to [Lower] California, having the desire . . . to put into execution projects whose bearing he considered to be of the greatest importance. . . .

Before giving an account of what was done by Don José de Gálvez, it is necessary to say something about the coasts of California . . . in order that . . . the scanty resources which could be relied upon in such distant regions should be made known. . . .

WEAK DEFENSES

The conquered part of California beginning from Cape San Lucas extended only as far as latitude 30° 30′ where is situated the Mission of Santa María at a short distance from the Bay of San Luis Gonzaga. . . . . But this whole country was inhabited by hardly anyone except its own natives, of whom only a few were collected in the missions.

. . . . The number of these natives is very limited, and with the exception of being baptized and made Christians, they preserve in everything the same mode of procuring their livelihood as in their savage state. . . .

The Spaniards and other races—spoken of in America as white people—who were settled in the peninsula did not number four hundred souls, including the families of the soldiers of the Presidio of Loreto, and of some men who called themselves miners. . . . From this may be inferred how little it would be possible to count upon the inhabitants of the country for the defense of its coasts, and the opportunity offered to any foreigners to establish themselves there without fearing the least opposition, especially if they had attempted to land toward the north in the celebrated ports of San Diego and Monterey. Such a contingency would have brought with it disastrous consequences, for they could have taken possession of the country and fortified themselves in those places without the knowledge coming to the attention of the [Spanish] government, or so late that the loss would be irreparable.

On the South Sea [Pacific], on all that part that touches upon the coast of New Spain, no vessels were known other than the packets recently built in San Blas, and two others of small tonnage. . . . These few ships constituted all the naval force that could be opposed to a foreign invasion. . . .

He [Gálvez] realized the necessity of settling the discovered part of California with industrious people capable of cultivating its lands . . . as well as of bearing arms in defense of their homes whenever the occasion should arise. Owing to the great extent of the territories comprised under the name of California . . . it was equally necessary to advance the new settlements as far north as possible which, by joining hands with those of the south, might afford mutual assistance.

[Costansó]

Following Vizcaíno's expedition in 1602, King Philip III had given royal orders for the occupation and settlement of Monterey. The port was needed as a rest station for the galleons returning on the slow, lumbering voyages from the Philippines when they might be seven to nine months at sea. They were loaded with the rich and exotic wares of the Indies, to be sold for an extravagant price, but the crew was so ill-supplied with food and water that countless died. It was to relieve this wretched state of affairs that Vizcaíno had been dispatched to discover a safe harbor along the upper coast of California. Plans to make use of it came to nothing, though missionaries clamored to be sent there, and a century and a half elapsed before a real move was made. The treasury of Spain was overtaxed, and religion was seldom advanced unless it was also part of a political scheme.

BEGINNING OF CONQUEST

Now Don José de Gálvez was the activator, and no man could have been better chosen for the role. The Inspector General had a mettle to match Padre Serra's, though of a different sort, and together they made a remarkable team. Gálvez had an intensity and drive that cut through official snags and brushed aside all man-made delays. If there were a job to do, his idea was to get on with it.

He decided that two types of expeditions would be essential to bring success to this ambitious project—one to go by land and one by sea, where the hazards were great. He well knew the mishaps that could attend a long ocean voyage on which the men might fall ill and the ship be driven far off course by the winds that prevailed along the coast of California.

In preparation and to save money, Gálvez ordered all the Lower California missions to contribute vestments and sacred articles for the proposed new missions, along with dried fruits, wines, salted meats, and other provisions that could be carried on muleback or in the holds of the ships *San Carlos* and *San Antonio*. These missions were also to supply horses and cattle which would accompany the land expedition that, for safety's sake, was divided into two companies, Gálvez was taking no chances so that at least one might survive to reach the first destination of San Diego. They would be breaking trail through what was largely unexplored country, and there was no foretelling whether the Indians would prove hostile.

One company was to be headed by Don Fernando de Rivera y Moncada, captain of dragoons, and the other by bluff, hearty Don Gaspar de Portolá, governor of Lower California. Between them, they would have

29

163 well-laden mules. Padre Serra was to go with Portolá, though there were serious doubts in all minds but his own whether he would be able to complete a journey that could run to one thousand miles. He was fifty-six years old, and the old pains had returned to his leg. It was feared he might have to travel by litter and that he would die somewhere along the rough trail.

During the past two years, the infection had been aggravated by his extensive travels up and down Lower California between the various missions in this rude, poverty-stricken land. Loreto, the capital where he had landed, was little more than a settlement of earth-built cabins and sheds on a sandy wasteland, though the humble mission here had many

Mission of Loreto.

paintings and handsome vestments left by the Jesuits. As the fourteen fathers scattered to their various posts, many were dismayed and discouraged, and it took Serra's spirit to rally them. The missions were strung out over five hundred miles, and visiting them on muleback and afoot had cost Serra a swelling that went halfway up his left leg.

Recently he had trekked nearly two hundred miles from Loreto to La Paz to confer with Gálvez, who was hastening preparations for the departure of the *San Carlos*. This was to be the first ship to sail for San Diego.

Beams loosened by heavy seas had to be calked while Gálvez, smeared with tar, worked side by side with the crew. He was equally energetic in loading the ship, helping Serra to pack the religious articles and urging the twenty-five passengers, including soldiers and missionaries, to share their excitement. Among them was Miguel Costansó. The *San Carlos* sailed early in January of 1769 after Serra had celebrated Mass in honor of St. Joseph, who had been chosen as patron saint of both sea and land expeditions.

On March 28, after Easter, Serra bid farewell to his Mission of Loreto and stopped a few days with Palóu at his Mission of San Francisco Xavier before continuing north to join Portolá. Their affection was deep, and they had much to talk about since, in the case of Serra's death or long absence, Palóu was to take his place as President of the Missions of the Californias. This could be their last meeting, and Palóu was profoundly concerned over the sad condition of his friend who was to travel into unknown territory for "the greater honor and glory of God and the conversion of the Infidels to our Holy Catholic Faith."

> When I saw him and his swollen foot and leg with its ulcer I could not keep back the tears when I thought of how much he still had to suffer in the rough and difficult trails . . . without other doctor or surgeon than the Divine aid and without other protection for his lame foot than a sandal, as he never would use anything else in all the journeys he took . . . saying that he could not use shoes or stockings or boots because it was better for him to have his leg bare.
>
> [Palóu]

Palóu told Serra that he might bring calamity upon the expedition or

Mission of San Francisco Xavier.

greatly delay it and offered to go in his place. Portolá also had his apprehensions, which he had expressed to Gálvez in the belief that the festering
was cancerous. To each of them, Serra replied that he was putting all his
trust in God to see him safe to San Diego and on to Monterey. Gálvez,
knowing his great spirit and iron determination, sided with the friar and
gave him his vote of confidence.

Lifted painfully on a mule by the two soldiers who escorted him, Serra
continued on his way from mission to mission until he reached the rendezvous with Portolá on the frontier. They penetrated new territory and
paused for several days at Velicatá while Portolá saw to the loading of the
packtrain and the rounding up of the cattle.

They built a rude little chapel, and here on May 14 Fray Junípero dedicated the first of the new missions to San Fernando and left a padre in charge. He also had time to write the last letters he would be able to send for an indefinite period.

AGONY OF PAIN

Before they had advanced many leagues, he was in an agony of pain from his leg that caused him even greater anguish of spirit. If he were to continue, it appeared that he would have to be carried on a stretcher by the converted Indians, an extra labor and a prospect that caused him deep distress. In desperation, he turned first to God and then with this inspiration to one of the muleteers, asking him to contrive some remedy such as he used to treat the gall sores on the backs of the pack animals.

The man laughed and said he was no doctor, but in order to please the good father sought herbs in a field. These he crushed between two stones with a mixture of tallow and applied it warm as a poultice. Serra slept well through the night and awoke nearly free from the pain. To him and to Portolá, his recovery seemed almost miraculous, and they took to the trail with the padre astride an old worn-out mule.

Ruins of San Fernando de Velicatá.

Geiger photo, Santa Barbara Mission Archives

Rivera had preceded them by several weeks with twenty-nine soldiers, and they were accompanied by ten in sleeveless leather jackets worn as a protection from Indian arrows. This armor was made of six or seven plies of white tanned deerskin that was impenetrable except at close range, like the raw bullhide shields they carried, while the horses wore leather aprons to guard their flanks. The soldiers were excellent horsemen capable of handling a lance at full gallop and a broadsword in closer quarters. These, with a short musket securely strapped in a case, completed their armament.

With the horses, troops of pack mules, and cattle they made a long and impressive cavalcade as they wound through the chaparral. These tangled and thorny thickets were cut for them by the converted Indians who preceded the train and who would also act as interpreters. Sergeant José Francisco Ortega was dispatched on ahead to explore for water holes and suitable camping places, though, as Portolá wrote in the *Diary* he kept, the search was often vain. In this hostile land of cacti and rattlesnakes, Portolá's terse day-to-day entries frequently mentioned "no pasture and no water for the animals . . . much pasture but no water for man or beast . . . the entire road over very rough slopes, and halted without either pasture or water."

Dust-parched throats often had little but the liquid from the heart of certain cacti to slake their thirsts, and there was small shade from the sun that beat ceaselessly day after rainless day from the cloudless sky. Green arroyos were as scarce as the groves of dwarfed trees that somehow manage to survive in this dry and desolate region.

Fortunately, neither the governor nor the friar in his tattered gray tunic were aware of the ill fate of the men aboard the *San Carlos* as they pushed steadily northward to join them at San Diego. Serra was in good health and spirits, never mentioning his leg again in the detailed *Diary* he kept and from which excerpts follow.

> May 23. . . . According to my calculations, we traveled four and a half hours; and for more than half that time the road was all steep hills, rocky and tiresome, up hill and down dale, till we came to some level mesas where we found evident signs that the first division of the land expedition had stopped there. We did likewise. As there was no water in sight, we dug a water hole for

the animals to drink. May 24. We resumed our journey. It lasted three hours and a half, following half the time a dry ravine with much sand, making the going heavy. There were a few palm trees. Then came ugly steep hills, leading to a plain encircled by mountains. . . . Water had been brought in skins for the men, but the animals did not have any. . . . The blazing sun made the journey very painful.

For the last four nights a roaring lion[puma] quite close by kept us awake. May God guard us from it, as He has till now.

Occasionally they would sight a few Indians naked as nature, but the "gentiles," as Fray Junípero termed them to distinguish them from Christians, were shy and they fled at their approach. Except for these two expeditions and one several years before by a Jesuit into part of this region, the natives had never seen white men, nor had they seen horses or mules. As Serra was later to discover, the California Indians came to the conclusion that the odd strangers must be the papooses of these large animals, since they were carried on their backs much as a squaw might transport her offspring.

Also, the Spaniards did not seem like other men because they had no women among them. The Indians suspected that these palefaces had come among them for the sole purpose of stealing their wives. This was a complication that would later cause serious problems, as Serra attempted to restrain the soldiers in the course of the conquest, but presently his chief concern was trying to make friends with the natives.

Finally they were able to capture an Indian, but he quivered with terror when Serra made the sign of the Cross over his head. They offered him figs, meat, and tortillas, and he ate a little "with great excitability."

INDIAN AMBUSH

All his talking seemed to be to excuse himself for having spied on us from the hill yesterday and today. . . . He told us he had been sent by his chief to spy upon us, the purpose being that, as we continued our march, the chief and all his *ranchería* [village] together with four other chiefs and their *rancherías* . . . lying in ambush behind the rocks, should surprise the Father and all accompanying him, and put them to death. . . . We pardoned him his murderous intentions, and loading him down with presents, we let him go in order that he might tell his people how well we treated him . . . that they, too, might come to see us. But not one came, although some were seen this afternoon on the same ridge. . . .

May 28. Sunday. Before our departure, some gentiles approached us belonging to the group our soldiers had seen while keeping guard over the animals. Their huts were about twelve in number. Immediately our converts joined them to bring them to us. This only excited their hostile demonstrations, and, time and again, they made as if to shoot their arrows . . . so indignant were they that we could not calm them.

The time for Mass has come, and in order to hear it the soldiers made a circle and put them seated in the middle. . . After Mass another large number of them came, and their shouting continued. . . There was no way we could quiet them or disperse them. What they said, according to our interpreters, was that we should not go farther but go back, and that they wanted to fight. . . . We spent much time patiently trying to send them away in a friendly way. It was all in vain, no use whatever, and we feared bloodshed. By order of the governor, four soldiers mounted on horses, forming a line, forced them to retreat. But they again refused to go. At first one and then, a little later, a second shot was fired into the air by a soldier. On hearing it, they fled. . . .

When we left today's stopping place, they followed us along the hills . . . so that during the whole day's trip we saw a great number of them continually running along the hills in the same direction as ourselves. However, to get near us they had to come down to level ground. . . . Matters were different, however, when the mountains came close together, and we had to pass between them through a narrow gully. All the soldiers then buckled on their leather jackets, and they and the mule drivers kept their arms ready for firing. We all kept on the alert, but the enemy did not show up. . . .

But as if to relieve us from the displeasure which they had caused us, Our Lord God sent us other Indians of a more pleasing character;

and so one league before arriving at our camping grounds, twelve new gentiles came to us. Very politely, they said they would show us the place. . . While we were busy with unloading . . . they retired to a nearby hillside and remained sitting there motionless. When we were free I sent them . . . an Indian interpreter, carrying presents of figs and meat, with an invitation to come and meet us without fear, since we were their friends. They replied showing they were highly delighted. . . And so it happened that after we had taken our meal and some rest, they came with . . . all their weapons which they laid on the ground. They started in to explain their use in battle, one after another. They played all the parts both of the attacker and the attacked in such a vivid way . . . that it was a pleasant relaxation for all of us. . . .

INDIAN WOMEN

So far we had not seen any woman among them, and, till now, I was anxious not to see them, because I feared they went as naked as the men. But when, in the midst of the entertainment, two women appeared—talking as rapidly and efficiently as that sex is accustomed to do—and when I saw them so decently covered that we would feel happy if no greater display of indecency were ever seen among the Christian women at our missions, I no longer regretted their arrival.

The younger of the two who was, they said, the wife of the chief, who also was there, carried upon her head the present [to us], the like of which I had never seen—a great pancake of a thing like dough, but full of thick fibers. I went to lay my hands upon her head, and she left the cake in my hands. She and her husband immediately began to explain to me how it was eaten. The older woman spoke also, yelling louder than the rest. . . .

ANIMAL STAMPEDE FEARED

May 29. At the beginning of today's march we came across, in a small plain, the little houses or huts of our friends the gentiles of yesterday afternoon . . . but now in greater numbers. They wanted to keep their promise to accompany us, and they came shouting at the top of their voices. However, as the road was bad and narrow, with all good intentions, they actually did us more harm than good, frightening the animals and almost making them bolt. We told them to quit. . . But in all the uproar they paid no attention nor did they hear us; and the commotion became worse as the road steadily became more dangerous. Their chief was called and made to understand the situation. He tried his best to quiet and recall his people, but was only partially successful. . . . Seeing that nothing else would do, he [Portolá] commanded a rifle to be fired into the air, and they were frightened and stopped. But I had my misgivings that, by such a display, we might leave in their minds some doubt as to our good will toward them.

[Serra]

Fears of an animal stampede—horses and mules alike plunging out wildly—were always present in such a cavalcade, as Costansó noted on a later land expedition.

The pack animals themselves constitute the greatest danger on these journeys and are the most dreaded enemy; though without them nothing could be accomplished. At night, and in a country they do not know, these animals are very easily frightened. The sight of a coyote or fox is sufficient to stampede them. . . . A bird flying past, or dust raised by the wind is likely to frighten them and make them run many leagues, throwing themselves over precipices and cliffs. . . .

Because of the rugged nature of the terrain and the size of their company, the Portolá party was seldom able to travel more than four or five hours before it halted and made early camp. As the land became more fertile and it seemed as though irrigation might produce good harvests, Serra was constantly on the look out for sites where new missions might stand. From the experience of his boyhood and later in the Sierra Gorda, he had acquired a practiced eye for animal husbandry and agriculture. Despite the fatigue and excitements of the day, he would explore with the Indian altar boy who attended him before he returned to his rest.

During the night he always slept with a large crucifix clasped in his hands and his breviary nearby where he could read in the first morning light. With the stirring of the camp, he would say Mass and celebrate such saints' days as might occur on the calendar. Even the rude soldiers felt his fervor as they stood with bowed heads. This was a Holy Mission; it must not fail.

Often they had to stop and rest for several days near some source of water, but finally Serra was able to note exuberantly in his *Diary* that he believed " the thorns and rocks of [Lower or Old] California have disappeared, since these enormous mountains are almost entirely of pure soil."

ROSE OF CASTILE

There are flowers in abundance and beautiful ones. . . And that there should be nothing wanting in that direction, when we came to our stopping place, we met the queen of flowers—the Rose of Castile. While I write this, I have in front of me a cutting from a rose-tree with three roses in full bloom, others opening out, and more than six unpetalled: blessed be He who created them!

We stayed in this place so that the animals might take advantage of the fine pasture and the water of the River of Roses. . . I saw so many rose bushes in flower that a purveyor of perfume could easily make a fortune. . . .

June 6. Today we see how much mistaken we were in believing that the peninsular sea was close to hand, for after all these days of travel we see before us ridge after ridge of high mountains so that the ocean to the west seems farther away every day.

[Serra]

The Pacific . . . San Diego . . . and then countless leagues farther by sailing vessel to Monterey to plant the flag of Spain beside the Cross. Though they might sigh at the view of these mountains, it was impossible to foresee all the other obstacles that lay between them and their goal.

IV   REUNION
"Some things must be suffered for God."

It was assumed that the men who came by sea would be well established in San Diego before either of the land expeditions arrived, but for this side of the tale we have the *Narrative* of Miguel Costansó aboard the *San Carlos,* which had left port a month ahead of the *San Antonio.*

> The navigation of the outer coast of California presents an unavoidable difficulty on account of the prevalence of north and northwest winds which, with little interruption, continue throughout the year, and are directly contrary to the voyage as the coast bears northwest to southeast. This makes it necessary for all vessels to keep away from the coast and gain sea room until they encounter more variable and favorable winds with which, making as far north as they require, they can stand to windward of the port for which they are bound. . . .
>
> The *San Carlos* encountered such great opposition from the winds and calms that it was driven to sea more than 200 leagues from the coast and, being short of water, had to make for the coast to procure some.

THE SCOURGE OF SCURVY

Water was procured with difficulty on Cedros Island, since the vessel had to tack between mainland and island and could find no place to drop anchor. Further, the water was soon found to be polluted, causing added distress. It was 110 days after leaving La Paz that the *San Carlos* finally reached San Diego with troops and crew in deplorable shape.

Scurvy had attacked all without exception owing to lack of fresh foods in their diet during their prolonged months at sea. They had been deprived of the all-important vitamin C; and, by the time they reached San Diego, two men had already died of this disease. The majority of the crew and half of the soldiers were incapacitated, confined to their beds in a misery of bleeding gums and muscular anguish.

Only four seamen were remaining on their feet, and they, assisted by the soldiers, had to trim and furl the sails and work the ship.

The packet *San Antonio,* although it sailed one month after the *San Carlos,* had the good fortune to complete the voyage in 59 days and had been in the Port of San Diego since the 11th. of April. But half its crew was likewise afflicted with the scurvy of which, also, two men had died. Amid so much sickness, all experienced great happiness at being reunited. . . . As soon as the *San Carlos* was moored to a suitable berth, the officers resolved by common consent to devote themselves to the immediate relief of the sick.

The first task was to look for a watering place where a supply of good water could be obtained to fill the barrels for the use of the men. For this purpose, the officers—Don Pedro Fages, Don Miguel Costansó, and the second captain of the *San Carlos*—landed on the 1st. of May with 25 of the soldiers and seamen who were best able to endure the fatigue.

[Costansó]

They saw Indians armed with bows and arrows who refused to be over-taken although the Spaniards hailed them with white handkerchiefs trying to obtain information.

Nor was it possible for our men to make greater speed because they were weak. . . . The Indians stopped from time to time on some height to watch our men, showing the fear which the strangers caused them by what they did to conceal it: they stuck one end of their bows into the ground and, holding the other end, danced and whirled around it with incredible swiftness.

[Costansó]

Finally the Spaniards were able to win over the Indians with presents of ribbons, glass beads, and other trifles. They were guided to the bank of a river three leagues distant which emptied into a lagoon where the ship's launch could go at high tide.

THE SAN DIEGO INDIANS

Within a musketshot of the river, they discovered a town or village of the same Indians who were guiding our men. It was composed of various shelters made of branches and huts, pyramidal in shape, covered with earth. . . Men, women, and children came out to receive them and invited the strangers into their houses. The women were modestly dressed, covered from the waist to the knee with a close-woven, thick netted fabric. . . .

These natives are well built, healthy, and active. They go naked without other clothing than a belt, woven like a net of *ixtle* or very fine agave thread. . . Their quivers, which they stick between the belt and the body, are made of the skin of the wildcat, coyote, wolf, or deer and their bows are two yards long. In addition to these arms they use a throwing-stick of very hard wood . . . which they throw edgewise, cutting the air with great force. . . . When they see a snake or other noxious animal, they throw the stick at it and generally cut the animal in two. As the Spaniards learned afterward from their continued intercourse with the natives, they are of an overbearing disposition, insolent, covetous, tricky, and boastful; and although they have little courage, they boast much of their strength, and consider the strongest to be the most valiant.

[Costansó]

Having found the watering place, the Spaniards returned to the vessels and sailed them as close as possible to the lagoon. This was performed with great toil, since the number of sick was growing daily, while those most seriously ill died.

HIGH DEATH TOLL

Close to the beach, on the east side of the port, a small enclosure was built with a parapet of earth and brushwood and mounted with two cannon. Some sails and awnings were landed from the vessels and, with these, two tents suitable for a hospital were made. On one side were placed the tents of the two officers, the missionaries, and the surgeon. When everything was ready to receive the sick, they were brought on shore in launches and were housed in the tent as comfortably as possible.

These measures, however, were not sufficient to restore their health; for medicines and fresh foods, most of which had been used up during the voyage, were wanting. . . .

In the barracks the cold made itself severely felt at night, and the sun by day: extremes which caused the men to suffer cruelly. Every day two or three of them died, and the whole expedition which had been composed of more than 90 men was reduced to only eight soldiers and as many sailors who were in a condition to assist in guarding the ships, handling the launches, protecting the camp, and waiting upon the sick.

[Costansó]

Nothing so far had been heard of the first land expedition under Rivera until the fourteenth of May, when the men and the packtrain were sighted. After exchanging salutes with volleys of gunfire, they ran forward to throw themselves into each other's arms.

The whole land expedition arrived without having lost a single man [except two of the converted Indians] or even carrying one person sick after a journey of two months although they were on half rations, and with no more provisions than three sacks of flour, of which each man received two cakes for his entire day's ration.

[Costansó]

They decided to move the camp closer to the river where there might be shade, but still the sick men did not improve. Soon it would be impossible for either of the two packets to leave the port for lack of crews to man them. They would be unable even to sail back to Gálvez with news of their plight.

Meanwhile the Portolá party was discovering ever-new barriers and counterbarriers to the Pacific. They were running across tracks and paths that showed the region to be populous with natives, but these did not lead them to the sea, as Serra wrote in his *Diary*.

43

Day by day this country seems to grow bigger and bigger with great walls and fortress-like bastions rising up to defend the west coast. They force us to make many detours, thus more than doubling the length of our march. For that reason today we have traveled mostly toward the west, hoping to reach the sea, but it continues to escape us. . . .

After midday, and after eating our dinner, at one fell swoop nine Indians who belonged to our company have deserted. . . . We sent men to go after them, but not even tracks could be found. Questioning those who still remained as to the cause of so unexpected an event, seeing that they were always given food and good treatment, and they had always given the impression of being well satisfied, the answer we got was this: that they did not know, but they rather suspected that, being near San Diego, they were afraid they would be forced to stay there without hope of returning to their own missions. May Our Lord God bless them for the services they have rendered us, and the way we will miss them in the future. [Only twelve Indians were now left to serve as laborers and interpreters.]

June 19. During today's march, one of the governor's servants, born in Genoa and a cook by profession, proved the strength of his sword's steel by running it through the buttocks of a burro, leaving it dead at his feet. It seems it got in his way, and brought his own animal to a standstill. Having taken the evidence of eyewitnesses . . . the governor deprived him of his job, stripped him of his arms, and condemned him to follow the expedition on foot. Furthermore, he fined him four times the price of the animal—that is, forty pesos.

They reached the Pacific on June 20, at a place their sea chart told them was La Ensenada de Todos Santos (All Saints' Cove), and, walking along the wave-pounded curve of the shore near the clear blue waters of a beautiful bay, pitched camp for a day of fishing and relaxation for the men and rest for the animals. Shortly thereafter they came upon "a large *ranchería* of gentiles."

Their fine stature, deportment, conversation, and gaiety won the hearts of all of us. They loaded us down with fish and abalones; they went out in their little canoes especially to fish for us; they put on their dances for our benefit and insisted that we sleep there two nights. . . . The mules alone excited their astonishment and a considerable amount of fear. . . . The women are very decently dressed, but the men are naked like the rest of them [some Indian men covered their bodies with mud on chilly mornings, washing it off as the day warmed]. . . . On their heads they wear a kind of circlet made of otter or other fine fur. Their hair is cut just like a wig and plastered with white clay, all done very neatly. May God make their souls attractive too! Amen.

After Mass there was an exchange of trinkets between the soldiers and gentiles, bartering pieces of white cloth—to which they are very partial—for basketfuls of fresh fish. In this they showed themselves to be real businessmen: if the piece of cloth was small, the amount of fish was less—with no arguing allowed. . . . I felt the greatest pity to see so many souls, so friendly as these gentiles were, and to have to leave them.

During the march we saw hares, rabbits, and herds of antelope. But far greater is the multitude of poor sheep going astray: gentiles in great numbers of both sexes and all ages. Not only do they not run away as those in the beginning, but they join us along the road as well . . . just as if we had been lifelong friends of the closest kind. I really do not have the heart to leave them that way. So I invite them all to come to San Diego. . . .

At the end of five hours—our stretch for today—we could see we had to make a drop so sheer and steep that just to look at it made you shiver. Everyone had to dismount. And so between walking, sliding, skidding, falling, and getting up again, we got down to a valley no less luxuriant than where we stopped last night. . . . We, who have seen so many Indians, have never before seen so many gathered in one spot. As to their attractiveness I cannot find words properly to express it. Not to mention an untold number of men, there came to sit in a circle around me a great crowd of women and children. One of them thought it would be amusing to give me her baby—a nursing child—to hold for a while. . . .

One thing about these poor Indians that causes misgivings, and that a person has to be on the lookout for when he goes among them, is their intense desire or mania for clothes or trinkets. . . Food hardly appeals to them, as they are sturdy and robust. . . . But to get hold of gaudily colored cloth or any kind of rags, they all but jump out of their skins—as the saying goes—or take any risk. When I offer them anything to eat, they usually want to make me understand, by clear gestures, that they . . . want my habit which they tug at by the sleeve. If I had given the habit to all who wanted it, there would be by this time a pretty large community of gentile friars.

June 27. During our march today, the gentiles gave us cause to fear they had some evil designs. They followed us in great numbers . . . dividing themselves in two parts, one on each side of the road. As they kept their bows and arrows ready in their hands, they might have attempted some hostile act. At the same time they left all their women with us. We could not get rid of them. . . Anything we said to them was answered by great roars of laughter; and all the time they ran along like deer. Added to this for a time not a single gentile man was to be seen. Then all of a sudden they appeared again and all together let out a mighty war whoop. . . .

Before long there came to us more and more gentiles—men, women and children—in such numbers I could scarcely count them. Their friendliness degenerated into familiarity. . . . If they saw us sitting, they sat near us; and always with the hope that we would give them anything they wanted, not being content with trifles. From me they wanted my habit; from the governor his leather jacket, his waistcoat, breeches, in short everything he wore. It was the same with everybody else. They even pestered me quite a bit in an effort to obtain my spectacles. One of them gave me to understand that he only wanted to borrow them in order to see what sort of thing they were. So I gave them to him. But God alone knows what it cost me to recover them once more because he ran away with them. [And the nearest shop for eye-glasses two thousand miles distant!] At last, after no end of trouble, I got them back after they had gone through

46

the hands of the women and of everyone who wanted them.

[Serra]

DIRE TIDINGS

They were nearing their destination, and shortly they were hailed by Ortega, who had pushed on ahead. He had returned with a party of soldiers and fresh mounts sent by Rivera from San Diego, bearing the disturbing news from that port. Portolá hastened forward while Serra continued more slowly with the mass of the cavalcade. He had already traveled nine hundred miles from Loreto, but there were still perilously steep ravines to block his path.

> They were all alike coming straight from the mountains. And although I continued to pray and resign myself to the will of God etc., I summoned up all my courage—because you were no sooner out of one ravine than you were in another, and each one was dangerous. At one time I asked the guides: "Is this the last one?" "There are plenty more to come" was the answer. . . . Anyway, like all things in this world, the gullies came to an end. We arrived at a gentile settlement, thickly populated. We were very tired and inclined to stop there. But we were told by the Sergeant [Ortega] that they were an insolent tribe.

[Serra]

On his previous ride northward with only one companion, Ortega had been in great danger when he resisted their attempts to steal his clothing, and they had sent women to seduce him. Now the party proceeded wearily and camped for the night in a safer place. They wished to arrive more fully rested at San Diego, and they had guides who knew "the direction of the port by the way the wind blew." Fray Junípero had been traveling for six weeks along an arduous trail when at last he arrived there on the first of July at high noon.

> It was a day of much rejoicing and merriment for all [padres, sailors, soldiers, and officials], because even the labors themselves which each one had suffered in their respective journeys gave occa-

47

sion for this through the relief of mutually relating them to one another. And although this kind of consolation would appear to be the solace of unfortunates, we ourselves considered that we were very happy thereby and gave great thanks to God, who after all had brought us together here.

[Serra]

Serra found the port of San Diego "beautiful to behold," and he was reunited with the friars who had come by ship and with Crespí, who had accompanied Rívera. On the next day, the Feast of the Visitation, a High Mass was sung in honor of St. Joseph, patron saint of both land and sea expeditions.

While Serra made the rounds of the hospital ministering to sick, lonely men, Portolá conferred with his officers and with the ship captains. Most of the Catalonian volunteers who had come on the packets were ill, and nearly the whole crew of the *San Carlos* was already dead. The tragedy complicated the chance of reaching Monterey, which was known chiefly by reports a hundred and fifty years old. The whole future of this pioneering venture that had been so boldly begun was now dark with uncertainty and doubt. With prayer, Fray Junípero turned it over to God.

V   THE MYSTERY OF MONTEREY

"Having a little tortilla and the wild herbs of the field, what more do we want?"

In his clear, well-formed script, Serra wrote almost immediately to Fray Juan Andrés, present Guardian of San Fernando College, and after giving an account of the ship disasters and deaths, declared that "here are no Apaches, and no enemies other than the spiritual ones." He concluded in a characteristically enthusiastic but realistic vein:

> I consider that the missions to be founded in these parts will enjoy many advantages over the old ones, as the land is much better and the water supply more plentiful. . . . To sum up, those who are to come here as missionaries should not imagine that they come here for any other purpose than to put up with hardships for the love of God and the salvation of souls. In a desert like this, it is impossible for the old missions to come to the help of the new ones. The distances are great and the intervening spaces peopled by gentiles. In addition to this, the almost complete lack of communication by sea makes it necessary that they endure, especially at the beginning, many and dire hardships. But to a willing heart all is sweet, *amanti suave est.*

FIRST LAND EXPLORATION OF NEW CALIFORNIA

Here Costansó picked up the account of these anxiety-wracked days in July.

> The governor [Portolá] was of the opinion that the unforeseen misfortune of the ships did not excuse him from continuing his

journey to Monterey by land, in view of the fact that all his soldiers and the rest of his men were in good health, and that he had in his division 163 mules laden with provisions. He also counted upon the supplies which the packet *San José* was to bring, as according to the arrangements and advices of the inspector-general [Gálvez], this vessel could be presumed to be on its way to the same destination. He therefore determined to continue his march in search of that port, without waiting until the season was too far advanced, so as to avoid the risk of the snows blocking passage across the mountains that might be encountered on the way.

The *San Antonio* was hastily dispatched with a small crew scarcely able to handle the sails, carrying letters and urgent messages of emergency to De Croix and Gálvez. By mid-July Portolá was ready to ride northward with the two army officers Costansó and Don Pedro Fages, followed by soldiers and muleteers with Rivera as captain of the rear guard. "El Viejo," as the soldiers affectionately called Serra, was too exhausted to continue by land and would wait for the expected arrival of the *San José* to make the journey to Monterey. The younger padres Juan Crespí and Francisco Gomez would go with Portolá as chaplains. Costansó gave a quick summary of the arrangements for the first overland exploration of New California [Upper].

> There was left at San Diego a guard [of eight soldiers] which seemed sufficient for the protection of the mission and the sick, with the surgeon, Don Pedro Prat, so that he might continue to attend them. An adequate number of horses and mules for the use of all was left behind. The reverend fathers Junípero Serra, Juan Vizcaíno, and Fernando Parron also remained to establish the new mission.

For provisions, the party of seventy-four men carried one hundred packs. This should supply them for six months in case no packet reached Monterey during that length of time, a prospect that seemed most unlikely. One important factor in making the expedition a success would be the leather-jacketed soldiers, *Soldados de Cuere*. Costansó observed them working incessantly, and he lauded this force, far from family and home and nameless to history.

> They are men of great fortitude and patience in fatigue; obedient, resolute, and active, and we do not hesitate to say they are the best horsemen in the world, and among those soldiers who best earn their bread for the august monarch whom they serve. . . .

> It must be borne in mind that the marches of this body with so great a train and so many obstacles, through unknown lands and breaking trails could not be long. Not to mention other reasons that made it necessary to halt and camp early. . . . Stops were made, as the necessity demanded, at intervals of four days more or less, according to the extraordinary hardships occasioned by the greater roughness of the road, the labor of the sappers [who cut the brush], and the straying of the animals.

Meanwhile, despite his fatigue, Serra lost no time in busying himself at San Diego, as Palóu recorded.

> That fervent zeal with which the heart of the Venerable Father Fray Junípero continually burned and glowed never allowed him to forget the principal reason for his coming here. This it was that, two days after the departure of the expedition, urged him to make a beginning of the mission at San Diego in the port of that same name. . . . He performed the act of its founding with a High Mass and the other usual ceremonies. . . . The date was July 16, on which day we Spaniards celebrate the Triumph of the Most Holy Cross. He trusted that, just as the Spaniards, in virtue of this sacred emblem, obtained that celebrated victory over the barbarous Mohammedans on that day in the year 1212, by raising the standard of the Holy Cross he would succeed in driving out the whole army of hell and subject to the sweet yoke of our holy Faith the barbarous pagans who inhabited this New California. . . .

> Together with the few persons who were still well, they were engaged in constructing primitive huts during those intervals free from the care of the sick. One of these structures was dedicated as a

Hubert A. Lowman, courtesy California Mission Trails Association, .

Mission of San Diego de Alcalá.

temporary church. After this the missionaries tried by means of gifts and kind treatment to attract the pagans who presented themselves. But since these did not understand our language, they paid attention to nothing else but to accepting what was given them, provided it was not food. Food they absolutely would not taste . . . they attributed the illness of the men to the food, which they had never seen. This was, without doubt, a singular act of the providence of the Most High God, for if they had readily become attached to our type of food, as they became enamored of our clothing, our own Spaniards would have died of hunger.

ATTACK ON SAN DIEGO

The Indians stole every article of cloth they could lay hands upon, and went to such an extreme that even the sails of the *San Carlos,* anchored in the harbor, were not safe.

One night they had rowed up to it in their tule-boats [made of rushes], and there they were found cutting off a piece of sail; on another occasion they did the same in regard to a cable which they wanted to take with them. It was therefore resolved to put aboard a guard of two soldiers from among the eight leather-jackets who had remained there, hoping that by reason of this threat they would be restrained. But the mission guard was decreased, and more so on feast days when it was necessary that two other soldiers should accompany the father who went to celebrate Mass on the ship, lest some insult should be committed by the pagans.

They observed all these activities sharply. They were ignorant of the force of firearms and trusted in the strength of their numbers, as well as in their arrows and wooden instruments, fashioned like sabers, which cut like steel. They also had instruments such as clubs or wooden mallets, by means of which they cause great damage. So they began to rob without fear. Realizing that this was not tolerated, they were willing to take a chance, and by putting all of us to death they would take home the spoils.

[Palóu]

They waited for a holy day when only four soldiers remained on shore, and the padres Serra and Vizcaíno had just finished giving Communion. Fully armed, they fell upon the poorly protected settlement. Hastily the four soldiers put on their leather jackets, but the blacksmith, who had no such protection, excelled them all in valor. Firing his gun, he ran about among the huts crying, "Long live the Faith of Jesus Christ, and may these dogs, enemies of that faith, die!"

Serra remained within the little church, praying that the lives of both Spaniards and Indians might be spared and fully aware that any moment might be his last. Raising the mat that served as a door, Vizcaíno's hand was pierced by an arrow.

While the battle, amidst terrible howling by the Indians, was going on, the servant Joseph María, who looked after the fathers, ran hurriedly into their hut and cast himself at the feet of our

Venerable Father and said: "Father, absolve me, for the Indians have killed me."

[Palóu]

Driven off by the fury and force of the Spaniards' gunpowder, the Indians finally retired, carrying away all their dead and wounded so that the number of casualties should be concealed. Three of the Spaniards and an Indian from Old California [Lower] had been wounded, but not seriously, and they kept the death of the servant boy a secret.

Serra insisted upon charity and forgiveness for the Indians who had tried to kill them all but who now had a new respect for the power of Spanish arms. The Indians were encouraged to bring in their wounded for treatment by the surgeon, and eventually Serra was able to communicate with a bright Indian lad. The padre desired to baptize some of the babies, and finally one was brought to him. A crowd of Indians came to watch the ceremonies, but just as he was about to pour the water over the infant's head, they snatched it away and ran, terrified, off to their villages. Serra was left standing with the silver shell in his hand, once more frustrated in his attempts to make a breakthrough with the Indians of San Diego.

These were isolated, discouraging months in a hazardous pioneering venture, but he was sustained by a sense of divine mission. His superb courage and the dynamic drive in his frail body refused to admit the possibility of ultimate failure. No ship came into the harbor to relieve the *San Carlos* with fresh crews and provisions. . . . Serra suffered from scurvy like the others . . . and no word came back from the land expedition, which was having its own set of misfortunes.

Near what is now the Santa Ana River, the Portolá party experienced the shocks of a severe earthquake that terrified the natives visiting their camp and bewildered the Spaniards. Convinced that volcanoes must lie in the mountains beyond, they attempted to stay close to the coast. All along the way the Indians had been numerous and friendly, but it was around the Santa Barbara Channel that they came upon natives who seemed far superior to the others and who lived in real towns. Notes on them occupied many pages of Costansó's *Diary*.

We counted as many as thirty large and capacious houses [in one

Mission San Diego.

of the villages], spherical in form, well built and thatched with grass.
. . . There could not be less than four hundred souls in the town.

These natives are well built and of a good disposition, very agile
and alert, diligent and skillful. Their handiness and ability were at
their best in the construction of their canoes made of pine boards.
. . . They handle these with equal skill . . . . and go out to sea in them
to fish, as they will hold eight to ten men.

The Indians presented the Spaniards with dozens of strings of fish, fresh
and dried, and in return were pleased to receive glass beads and trinkets.
The chiefs from the various *rancherías* vied for their favor, and one day a
big crowd decked out in paint and feathers assembled to dance.

55

The dancing continued all afternoon, and we had hard work to rid ourselves of [our visitors]. . . . Finally we sent them away, earnestly recommending them, by means of signs, not to come back during the night and disturb us; but in vain. At nightfall they returned with a large retinue of clowns or jugglers, playing whistles, the noise of which grated on our ears. It was to be feared that they would stampede the horses. . . . [We] gave the natives some glass beads, and intimated that if they came back to disturb our sleep, they would no longer be our friends, and we would give them a bad reception.

[Costansó]

RUGGED TRAIL BLAZING

Day after day the cavalcade struggled across rocky arroyos and through brown sun-scorched hills with Monterey as the goal. They were breaking trail through rough terrain, and some were still so weak from scurvy that they scarcely could remain on their mounts until nightfall. Coming upon a valley that seemed to offer smooth going, they saw that it was riddled with holes. Proceeding cautiously lest the horses and mules break their legs, they came upon a troop of huge bears. Some of the soldiers decided to charge these grizzlies, who had been clawing up the ground in their search for edible roots.

They, however, experienced the fierceness and anger of these animals—when they feel themselves to be wounded, headlong they charge the hunter, who can escape only by the swiftness of his horse. . . . Their endurance and strength are not easily overcome, and only . . . the good fortune of hiting them in the head or heart can lay them low at the first shot.

[Costansó]

Striking toward the sea, the party was traveling up the coast when they were confronted by lofty mountains that marked the beginning of what is famous today as the Big Sur country. They concluded that this must be the Sierra de Santa Lucía named on the old maps, and beyond them they would find Monterey. Climbing day after day through narrow gorges and beside precipices "capable of frightening even the wild animals that lived there," they reached the highest peak only to gaze upon what seemed endless mountains. It was, as Crespí remarked, "a sad spectacle for poor travelers worn out by the fatigues of so long a journey."

ELUSIVE MONTEREY

Finally they reached a river and, following along its course, rested from their extreme exertions in camp. They could hear the sounds of the ocean but could not see the shore. Scouts were sent out under Ortega to reconnoiter and came back with disturbing reports. They had seen the landmarks such as the Punta de Piños, shown on the hundred-and-seventy-year-old charts made by the Manila galleon pilot Cabrera Bueno, but they enclosed no great protected port. Where was Monterey?

Could the ancient instruments have been misleading as to its latitude? If this were indeed Monterey, the *San José* should be anchored there, keeping the rendezvous. They had been led to expect a magnificent harbor and shores green with grass, and hospitable natives, but this was desolate, deserted country. As Costansó wrote: "Some began to suspect that we might have left behind us the port we were seeking, by reason of the great circuit we had made in passing through the mountain range."

They had been on the trail for eighty-three days. Ignorant of the climate, they could also assume by the calendar that winter was about to close in on them with freezing snows. The weather had grown chill with fog. With true Spanish devoutness, they turned to heaven for guidance, as Crespí recorded in his *Diary*.

> We constructed an arbor in which to celebrate the holy sacrifice of the Mass, which we [he and Gómez] both said with all possible devotion, begging the Holy Ghost . . . to give light to these men so that they might decide what is best to be done for the greater honor and glory of our king.

Following the Mass, Portolá called a meeting of his hardy officers and the two courageous padres to determine the course best to follow in this impasse. The date was October 4; Costansó's *Diary* read:

> He drew attention to the scarcity of provisions that confronted us; to the large number of sick we had among us (there were seventeen men crippled and unfit for work); to the season, already far advanced;

and to the great sufferings of those who remained well, on account of the unlimited work required in looking after the horses and watching them at night; in guarding the camp; and in the continual excursions for exploration and reconnaisance. . . . All the officers [and the two friars] voted unanimously that the journey be continued [north] as this was the only course that remained, for we hoped to find— through the grace of God—the much desired port of Monterey, and in it the packet *San José* which would relieve our needs. If God willed that in the search for Monterey we should all perish, we would have performed our duty toward God and man, laboring together until death for the success of the undertaking on which we had been sent.

The sick had to be carried on litters as they crossed hills that grew increasingly higher, sometimes with ponds between them. Often Indians fled, terrified, at the party's approach. The natives were small help for information or exploration, and the Spaniards had no tents to protect them from heavy rains. Fearing for the lives of the sick, they were surprised when the showers relieved much of their pain.

Saturday October 28. We did not know what to think of the indications: we were already above 37° 20′ north latitude without being certain whether we were distant from or near Monterey. We experienced frequent rains; our provisions were running short; we had our men reduced to the simple daily ration of five tortillas made of flour and bran; we had neither grain nor meat (four packages that remained were reserved for the sick). It was resolved to kill the mules in order to provide rations for the soldiers, but they put off this expedient until a time of greater need as, now and then, they would kill some ducks, and as all willingly ate the pinole and seeds which we obtained from the Indians but only in small quantities.

[Costansó]

With such a diet, the commander and most of the men developed dysentery but, as Costansó wrote, "There is no bad from which good does not come."

This was what principally brought about the relief of the sick. The change of season, the cessation of the northwest winds and fogs, and the beginning of the land breezes, which blew after the rainy season, contributed to the same result. The swelling and contraction of the limbs, which made the sick like cripples, disappeared little by little. At the same time their pains left them, and all symptoms of scurvy disappeared: their mouths became clean, their gums solid, and their teeth firmly fixed.

[Costansó]

DISCOVERY OF SAN FRANCISCO BAY

They had no inkling that they were on the verge of one of the most notable discoveries in the history of North American exploration. They were to be the first white men to gaze upon the glittering sweep of the great bay of San Francisco. Its existence had never been suspected by earlier navigators, who had seen only the small harbor under Point Reyes and had given the saint's name to it.

It was not until later that the magnitude and significance of their discovery of the world's greatest landlocked harbor dawned upon them. Now it only filled them with perplexity. This was just such a protected expanse as they had been led to picture for Monterey, and yet all signs and the latitude pointed to it as San Francisco. They were worn to the bone and half-famished—perhaps no major discovery ever met with a more lackluster and disappointed reception. Neither the diaries of Costansó or Crespí showed exultation; they merely recorded the facts.

October 31. . . . As soon as we ascended to the summit we descried a great bay formed by a point of land which runs far out into the open sea and looks like an island. Farther out . . . six or seven white *farallones* [rocky islands] of different sizes were to be seen. Following the coast of the bay to the north some white cliffs are visible, and to the northwest is the mouth of an estuary which seems to penetrate into the land. In view of these signs, and of what is stated in the itinerary of the pilot Cabrera Bueno, we came to the recognition of this port; it is that of Our Father San Francisco, and we have left that of Monterey behind. Filled with these doubts and arguments,

59

we descended from the hill and pitched camp in the middle of a small valley.

[Crespí]

Costansó wrote in the same vein, but there were many in the party who remained incredulous. This *had* to be Monterey. To avoid mutiny, Portolá sent out scouts to examine the land and return with more information.

November 3. . . . During the night the scouts returned to camp firing salutes with their arms. . . The reason for their demonstration of joy was none other than that they had inferred from the ambiguous signs of the natives that two days' march from the place at which they arrived was a port with a vessel in it. Upon this simple conjecture, some of them had finally persuaded themselves that they were at Monterey, and they had no doubt that the packet *San José* was awaiting us in that place.

[Costansó]

Following along the shore of the magnificent estuary whose entrance was later to be called the Golden Gate, they searched in vain. The scouts confessed that they had been misled, and officers and padres concurred in the decision to turn dejectedly south again and somehow find Monterey.

November 27. . . . We pitched our camp in sight of Punta de Piños.
November 28. We broke camp this morning and, keeping near the coast, began to ascend the hill of the pines. . . . We passed to the other side of the hill where a bay lies sheltered to the north and northwest. . . . This bay has to the south another point which protects it from the south and southwest. We cannot say that the anchorage protected by these points is good, as many flat stones and rocks can be seen in the water and on the shore . . . . nor [without boats] can we say what the character of the bottom of this bay is, nor what its depth may be.

[Costansó]

"DISAPPOINTED AND DESPAIRING"

They explored to exhaustion, but saw only a bay instead of the splendid safe harbor glorified in the minds of the Spaniards. On December 5, Costansó expressed the utter frustration of the whole company.

> We did not know what to think of the situation. A port so famous as that of Monterey, so celebrated, and so talked of in its time by energetic, skillful, and intelligent men, expert sailors who came expressly to reconnoiter these coasts by order of the monarch who at that time governed the Spains—is it possible to say that it has not been found after the most careful and earnest effort, carried out at the cost of so much toil and fatigue? Or is it admissible to think that it has been filled up, or destroyed in the course of time?
>
> . . . . On the return [of the scouting party] from the examination of the mountain range, our commander laid before his officers the unhappy plight in which we were placed—without provisions other than sixteen sacks of flour, without hope of finding the port and consequently of finding the ship which might aid us. . . .
>
> [After much discussion and several days] the commander himself resolved on the return [to San Diego]—in view of the few provisions that remained, the excessive cold, and, above all, the snow that was beginning to cover the mountain range . . . believing that if the passage over the mountains became impossible, we should all perish.

Raw stormy weather set in with huge waves pounding in from the sea. Their minds were also in tumult as they prepared to depart.

> Sunday December 10. Before leaving this bay we erected a cross upon the beach with an inscription cut upon the wood which said: "Dig! At the foot thou wilt find a writing."

It told the whole story of the expedition and its vain attempts to find Monterey. In the event that either the missing *San José* or possibly the *San Antonio* should land and read the message, a request was made that they follow along the coast and somehow make communication with the land party to save it from starvation. The ending was poignant.

> Finally now disappointed and despairing to find the port after so

many endeavors, labors, and hardships and without other provisions than fourteen sacks of flour, the expedition sets out today for San Diego. Pray thou Almighty God to guide it, and, sailor, may his Divine Providence take thee to a port of safety.

[Costansó]

VI   TRIUMPHANT BELLS

"For the kingdom of God, some boldness is more in keeping than all these cautions they are forever urging on me."

Six months previously, the Portolá party had marched north with a confident step, but now they were straggling southward uncertain even as to the fate of San Diego. They were ravenous, and by December 20 only enough flour remained to provide each man with a total of five thin tortillas for the rest of the journey. Occasionally they feasted on fish or bear meat, but shortly they were driven to killing the mules. Apprehensions nagged them as much as the emptiness of their stomachs, as Crespí noted in his diary entry of January 24, 1770.

We were now approaching the port of San Diego, and this whole day was passed in conjecturing what state we would find it in, whether settled by the few people whom we left there and the packets in the harbor, or whether it might have been entirely deserted in the six months since we had left it. Each one decided according to his nature and humor; but it is true that we all agreed in the fear that if the rigor of sickness and mortality among the people had lasted, not a span of the establishment would be left standing. . . .

Occupied by these thoughts and remarks, which had fatigued us for some days, we at last made out the fence of poles and the humble buildings that contained the mission. Immediately all the soldiers discharged their firearms, our first announcement to the inhabitants of the mission who, in the greatest excitement, came out immediately to receive us with open arms.

Though he was still weak from scurvy, Serra was jubilant. Not a man had died on the land expedition, despite excruciating privation, and this called for a Mass of profound thanksgiving. Some of the Indians had deserted along the way, but sixty men had returned.

To be sure, they had not found Monterey, but they had gone on to discover a great bay that was apparently San Francisco. Always optimistic, Serra considered this to be clear proof that they had been led by Divine Providence. Months before they started the conquest, he had told Palóu of Gálvez' prophetic remark:

"If St. Francis wants a Mission, let him cause his port to be discovered and a Mission for him shall be placed there."

[Palóu]

Though Fray Junípero had been unable to make a single convert, it was not in his character to admit of defeat, and he was convinced that Monterey could be located. He still envisioned a whole chain of missions, while Portolá faced the harsh realities of their situation. The *San José* had vanished without a trace, and they could only assume now that it had been lost at sea. The *San Antonio* was long overdue on its return voyage—the silence from Mexico was like that of a tomb. With sixty additional mouths to feed, the scanty corn, flour, and grain at San Diego would soon be exhausted, and shortly he dispatched Rivera to Old California with forty of the men. The urgency was extreme, and he was making a last call for help.

NEW CALIFORNIA TO BE ABANDONED

Portolá was a brave commander, but he thought he would only discredit himself and risk starvation for his whole company by a venture that seemed hopeless. To him the wise course was to abandon the conquest of New California as soon as they could pack up and leave.

Serra pleaded with him to wait. Was it possible that they had been entirely deserted in this remote outpost by the high command of New Spain? With such arguments and with his own fervor, Serra bolstered Portolá's stand against the discouraged lonely men, who were angrily pressing for immediate departure, and prevailed upon his piety to remain until March 19. This marked the feast day of St. Joseph, their patron saint, to whom they would hold a novena, and it would be positively the final date.

Fray Junípero was in a state of acute anguish. No one knew when the little padre slept or what he ate as he tried to hold to his faith in earthly powers while he prayed to those of heaven. He foresaw clearly that, if the project were now to be abandoned, Spain might never again make another attempt on these shores. The effort had been heroic and so costly in terms of money and men that centuries might pass before it was revived. Spain could not afford to back further defeats; it required triumphs. Palóu told of his state of mind.

All these conversations and preparations were so many arrows that pierced the fervent heart of our Venerable Father President, who in his holy prayers incessantly commended this affair to God, begging that the ship would arrive before the day assigned for the expedition's departure. This he asked for, lest the opportunity be lost for converting to God so many pagan souls which were at hand.

Whatever took place, Fray Junípero determined to remain behind, perishing with the last tortilla if need be. As he had written to his parents years before when leaving for the Indies, one must always go forward and never turn back. With passionate resolution, he now took action, as Palóu related.

He went out to the ship to confer on this matter with the sea commandant, Don Vicente Vila, and spoke to him in this way: "Sir, the governor, who is land commander, has decided to go back, abandoning this port by the 20th. of this month, if neither of the ships should arrive by that time with relief. The lack of provisions and the common opinion that the Port of Monterey has been filled up [with sand] force him to this action. I suspect, however, that they did not recognize it."

"I think likewise," said the commandant, "from what I have heard them say and from what I have read in their letters, namely that the port is located right there where they have planted the cross."

"Well then, Sir," said the Venerable Father, "I have determined to stay here even though the expedition departs. Father Crespí will keep me company. If you so permit, let us come out here to you, as soon as the expedition leaves, and when the other packet boat arrives we shall go up in it in search of Monterey."

65

The captain agreed willingly, and they decided to keep the arrangement a secret between them.

A SAIL! A SAIL!

St. Joseph's feast day arrived, and High Mass was celebrated with the full splendor of the silver vessels and ecclesiastical robes brought from Mexico. In his sermon, Fray Junípero attempted to fire the assembled company with his own burning faith, but other hearts faltered. They had seen no sign, and tomorrow they would begin their retreat southward.

It was not until late afternoon that the settlement was aroused with a cry. All rushed out to see a sail disappearing over the horizon like a sea gull in flight. A sail! A sail! . . . the first in ten brutal months.

Helplessly they watched while the vision vanished, but Portolá postponed his plans to abandon San Diego. What seemed like a miracle took tangible form four days later when the *San Antonio* swept into port. It had been on its way to Monterey to succor the land expedition, but chance (or the power of St. Joseph) made it turn back. Stopping in the Santa Barbara Channel for fresh water, the crew had been informed by Indian pantomime that Portolá had gone south. The natives had climbed on barrels to imitate the action of men on horseback, but still the Spaniards had been afraid to credit this information. Captain Pérez had his orders to proceed directly to Monterey, but while he was getting under full sail he lost one of his anchors. He had no choice then but to change course and come around to borrow one from the *San Carlos*.

Now Portolá had ample provisions to make a second journey by land while the *San Antonio* went by sea. Between the two expeditions, the Spaniards were confident that Monterey could no longer elude them.

"Long live Jesus, Mary, and Joseph!" Serra's salutations in letters written aboard the *San Antonio* could ring with exuberance. She had set sail for the north on April 16. Carried off course by contrary winds and bad weather, the ship took forty-six days for its voyage, while the land party arrived in thirty-eight. Crespí had gone with Portolá, and he recorded the historic meeting.

> On the 31st of May in the afternoon, a week after our arrival, the bark was seen very close to the Punta de Piños, and soldiers went to

signal to it that we were already there. It saluted us with cannon shots to let us know that it recognized us, and then came in to the very spot where the cross was, entering like Pedro into his own house, guided by the very same anchorage and signs given in the histories.

Why had Portolá been unable to recognize a port that had been right at his feet? His search had been conscientious, but his view from land had been vastly different from one from the sea. Reality did not compare with the myth that had grown in men's minds about Monterey. It was believed to offer fabulous scope and protection from storm. In short, the port had been over-advertised. Furthermore, the sea-tossed mariners of old had seen a shore brightened by winter rains and painted with wild flowers, while the Carmel was a rushing river. Portolá had arrived at the brown parched end of the dry season when the Carmel was little more than a creek. Nor had he had a ship to take depth soundings and prove it was still an excellent harbor. Now victory was to be celebrated, as Serra described in his *Writings;* Spain was taking possession of Monterey.

"LONG LIVE THE FAITH! LONG LIVE THE KING!"

The day came. A little chapel and altar were erected in that little valley, and under the same live-oak close to the beach where, it is said, Mass was celebrated at the beginning of the last century. Two processions from different directions converged at the same time on the spot, one from the sea, and one from the land expedition; we singing the divine praises in the launch, and the men on land in their hearts.

Our arrival was greeted by the joyful sound of the bells suspended from the branches of the oak tree. Everything being in readiness and having put on alb and stole, I intoned the hymn *Veni, Creator Spiritus,* at the conclusion of which, and after invoking the help of the Holy Spirit on everything we were about to perform, I blessed the salt and the water. Then we all made our way to a gigantic cross which was all in readiness and lying on the ground. With everyone lending a hand we set it in an upright position. I sang the prayers for its blessing . . . And thus, after raising aloft the standard of the King of Heaven, we unfurled the flag of our Catholic Monarch like-

67

wise. As we raised each one of them, we shouted at the top of our voices: "Long live the Faith! Long live the King!" All the time the bells were ringing, and our rifles were being fired, and from the boat came the thunder of big guns.

[Serra]

In the midst of this wilderness two thousand miles from civilization, the sun shone upon a dazzling scene. It glinted from the gold threading the folds of Fray Junípero's vestments to the colors of the Persian rug on which he knelt and passed on to illumine the face of Our Lady of Bethlehem. This large and exquisitely carved wooden statue of the Virgin, dressed in the elegant robes of a lady of the court and wearing a high golden crown, can still be seen today at the Mission of Carmel. Navigators and sailors looked upon her as their special protector, and she had been wrapped as a precious parcel and sent on by Gálvez. He had rechristened her La Conquistadora and loaned her to take part in this triumph of Spain.

The rude soldiers kneeling in formation raised their bowed heads to view her seraphic face and sing with Fray Junípero *Salve Regina.* "May God be thanked for all things," Serra wrote, going on to describe the more worldly events of June 3, 1770.

> .... the officers proceeded to the act of taking formal possession of that country in the name of His Catholic Majesty, unfurling and waving once more the royal flag, pulling grass, moving stones, and other formalities according to law—all accompanied with cheers, ringing of bells, cannonades etc. In addition there was a banquet served afterward to all of us gathered together on the beach; later a walk at sunset along the ocean concluded the celebration, when the men of the land expedition returned to their Carmel [River], and we to the boat.

Costansó could now conclude his own *Narrative* with ringing sentences:

> This enterprise, desired for so many years and attempted many times with great preparation and costs, will doubtless be very acceptable to the august monarch who wears the crown of Spain. His generous heart Heaven rewards by arousing in his glorious reign great and illustrious men of all estates—ecclesiastical, military and politi-

La Conquistadora.

cal—who vie with one another and are equally zealous in the discharge of high responsibilities confided to their eminent capacities and talents, which are never employed more worthily in furthering the extension of the gospel and the public welfare of his loyal and devoted subjects.

Monterey was to be the capital of New California and the center for Serra's operations. Within a week, the little padre had taken stock of the site and decided for many reasons that the permanent location of the mission might have to be elsewhere. He was reporting to the Guardian of San Fernando College and did not neglect to cover practical essentials.

> Our great need now is candles for Mass; inner tunics, because it is very cold here; and, as I said before, on another occasion, two good blankets with markings on the material, indicating the name of each of the two new missions, and of the third one which I hope will be founded before long. Two with "San Diego;" two with "Monterey;" and two with "San Buenaventura" so that it may be known they are always to remain in their respective missions. Some chocolate which until now we have not run short of . . . Also plenty of woolens, cloths, and flannel stuff to cover in some sort this multitude of poor naked people who here are so docile and tractable.

He would need more missionaries, but they must be men of a heroic mold to match the tasks they faced. He had had unfortunate experience with some who had been among the first arrivals.

> I must insist that they not be men who put on a glum face whenever there is work to be done, and are scarcely here before they become dissatisfied and anxious to return to the College.
> Hardships they will have to face—these men who come to sacrifice themselves in so holy an enterprise—as everyone knows. And, although I am not going to shed a lot of tears on the subject, it is childish to pretend that what I have had to put up with, and what I now endure, is any mere trifle. Where distances are so great, hardships must be faced. And they are felt all the more keenly by one who is unwilling to be deprived of anything. However, I do not like to think that any of those who are coming are of such poor clay.

The first buildings to be erected at Monterey were warehouses to store the supplies carried in the hold of the *San Antonio,* which was soon to sail back to San Blas. Though the soldiers heartily disliked building construction, they were enlisted to cut the timber and transport it by muleback. Meanwhile Serra pondered how he might celebrate the Feast of Corpus Christi with brilliant pageantry. He had few wax candles to spare, and these would be blown out by the wind. Then, on the day before the Feast, he made an unexpected discovery on shipboard, as he wrote to Gálvez:

> . . . even if the angels did not bring them to us, at least they were obtained . . . as if sent to us, when a large box was opened aboard ship, which appeared to be a chest of medicine which the men were looking for, was found to contain lanterns of glass, never used before and of which no one knew anything.

Leafy green branches were arched across the ceiling of one of the warehouses among the banners of various saints while lanterns stood upon either side. A solemn processional, lit by more lanterns carried aloft, moved toward the altar, on which stood six great silver candlesticks and the statue of La Conquistadora. Even under the primitive conditions of a new country, Fray Junípero could achieve grandeur and pomp. Bells rang, cannons boomed, and friars and soldiers lifted their voices and their hearts in hymns of glory.

The original silver that Serra brought with him from Mexico.

The only thing lacking for our complete satisfaction was the presence of Your Illustrious Self [Gálvez]. If only you could have witnessed it through some little window.

[Serra]

CELEBRATION IN MEXICO CITY

When news of the successful occupation of Monterey reached Mexico City two months later, it caused a sensation.

So important for the greater glory of God, the diffusion of our holy Catholic Faith in the most northern part of California, and the honor of our Catholic Monarch, did His Excellency the Viceroy, Marqués de Croix, and the Illustrious Visitor General, Don Joseph de Gálvez, consider the establishment of Monterey, that they did not contain in their noble hearts the great joy which they experienced on August 10, 1770, with the news of the founding at that port of the Mission and Presidio of San Carlos; and they ordered the fact published in the populous City of Mexico, capital of New Spain. They requested the Dean of the Cathedral to order a solemn ringing of the cathedral bells, to be followed by those of all the other churches. . . . This caused general delight in all the inhabitants.

[Palóu]

This victory of Spain was printed in an account that was widely circulated and which called attention to the high esteem in which Their Excellencies held Fray Junípero as an "exemplary and zealous missionary." Their respect for his dedication and his abilities would give him the strong support he would require in further setbacks and conflicts.

Now it was with regret that Serra lost sight of Portolá, who sailed from Monterey with Costansó on the ninth of July, leaving the lieutenant Don Pedro Fages in command. The bluff hearty governor had accomplished his work here and was returning to Mexico as a hero, but he had been a good friend to the friars. They had worked well together, and Crespí paid tribute to the companion of many a desperate march.

Señor Don Gaspar de Portolá has comported himself toward everybody with much circumspection and prudence, and I do not know that the wisest could have done better with everybody, officials and soldiers. He has looked after us friars with the greatest kindness. . . .

Don Pedro Fages' capacities for leadership were an unknown quantity still to be tested—tested finally beyond every shred of Fray Junípero's patience—in the struggle to extend the California missions and bring thousands of Indians into the fold. It was human relations, the tug of war between purposes and personalities, that would be a far greater danger to the mission system in New California than the masses of Indians who could have destroyed it overnight.

Portolá was too good a man to be spared longer to these remote shores, and he left with La Conquistadora who would be hailed with festivities in Old California (no dancing was Serra's plea). It was only later that this treasured image of the Virgin would find a permanent resting place at Carmel.

The infant settlement could expect no further communication with New Spain for at least a year, when one of the ships might return with letters, news, and provisions. It was on its own with only forty men for protection and survival, including the padres and the Old California Indians. San Diego was four hundred and fifty miles to the south, and it had been left with a mere twenty-three men. The Spanish treasury was dwindling, and a token force was expected to begin the civilization of New California.

SUPERNATURAL POWERS

Here in Monterey, Fray Junípero could depend upon the assistance of supernatural powers that had already impressed the Indians who were scattered inland but often came to the shore. Upon his return to Monterey, Crespí had noted curious signs around the cross erected on his first journey.

> We found the cross surrounded on all sides by arrows and little branches with many feathered crests, stuck up in the ground, which had been put there by the gentiles. There was also a string of sardines still somewhat fresh hanging from a branch by the side of the cross, on another was a piece of meat, and at the foot of the cross there was a little pile of mussels.

The Indians had been greatly frightened by the discharge of artillery which accompanied the occupation of Monterey, but gradually they began to draw near as Padre Serra tried to win them with little gifts. He found them far more responsive than the natives around San Diego, and, when he and Crespí had learned enough of their language to be able to talk with them, they discovered the reasons for their tributes.

> ... the natives on several occasions declared the following: the very first time they saw our people the Indians noticed that all the Spaniards bore on their breasts a very resplendent cross; and when the Spaniards went away from there, leaving that large cross by the beach, the Indians were filled with such fear that they did not dare to approach so sacred an emblem. For they saw the cross shining with bright rays at a time when the rays of the sun which illumined the day were gone and were replaced by the shadows of night. They noticed, however, that the light of the cross grew so bright that it seemed to them to reach to the very heavens. On beholding it during the day without these phenomena, and in its natural size, they approached it and tried to win its favor lest they suffer any harm, and in deference to it they made their offerings of meat, fish, and mussels. When to their surprise it did not consume what they offered, they placed before it feathers and arrows, showing thereby they desired peace with the Holy Cross and with the people who had erected it there.

> [Palóu]

New California had the densest Indian population in North America (an estimated 100,000 to 150,000). On the whole, their way of life was simple and uncomplicated and had suited their needs for many centuries. They impressed the Spaniards generally as a happy race.

While some of these Indians were tall and handsome, the majority were short, flat-nosed, and broad-faced, without the proud bearing that characterized other tribes. Yet they were sturdy, strong, and intelligent, skilled in several important respects. Their baskets were of extraordinary intricacy and beauty, and they had discovered how to leach tannic acid from the acorns of the live oaks and thus make them a basic food. Without iron or any other metal to work with, they contrived cutting tools of flint and shells, and they were extremely clever at stalking game.

Owing to the mild climate and the comparative ease of finding food in all seasons, they did not have to fight nature to stay alive. When they were not hunting or fishing, it was common for the men to sleep sixteen hours a day while the women did all the work. They gathered the acorns and ground them into meal in their stone *metates,* and waded in the ocean at low tide to dig up shellfish and pry mussels from the rocks. When their brush huts became so filthy and crawling with vermin that even they could not endure them, they set fire to them and built new ones.

Along the Santa Barbara coast, where Padre Serra hoped to found the mission of San Buenaventura, the Indians had a more advanced culture, but now he had to work with the human material he found around Monterey. Teaching these people to labor here and at the long chain of missions he wished to establish was in itself an extraordinary challenge for a man of fifty-eight.

> . . . in order to accomplish such important projects, there was need that many workers of the Gospel come, supplied with vestments of all sorts, sacred vessels for the church, utensils for the house, and implements for the field. These were needed to accustom the newly baptized to the cultivation of the soil, that with the fruits they would thereby reap they could maintain themselves as human beings and not like birds, which they imitated in collecting the wild seeds produced by nature. The Indians would at the same time learn culture and progress.
>
> [Palóu]

VII   THE PADRE AND DON PEDRO

"Evils unless uprooted at the beginning are most difficult to cure."

Fray Junípero could foresee a hundred missionaries working in this vast new field of heathendom; neither he nor the viceroy nor Gálvez were men to make puny plans. Serra was in no frame of mind to be frustrated by the fussiness and regimentation of Don Pedro Fages, whom he called privately "the little molester." The lieutenant was efficient, and within a few months he had built a presidio of adobe, a rude house for himself, and a friary of plastered whitewashed palisades roofed with earth. Serra did not relish his proximity to a commander who tried to keep the key to their enclosure "so as to lock us in and out when he pleased," and he was upset when Fages forced the soldiers to work on Sundays. Furthermore, he did not wish to expose the Indians to the vices of the soldiers and discouraged the natives from congregating where their women could be seduced. He was anxious to establish a permanent mission elsewhere, as he had written shortly after his arrival at Monterey.

> There is no *ranchería* in the vicinity of this port, because of which, if the Indians are determined to embrace our holy Faith, we foresee a special difficulty in having them settle here. It might be necessary to leave the presidio and together with a guard change the site of the mission toward the area of Carmel [five or six miles away], a locality indeed delightful and suitable because of the extent and excellent quality of the land and the water supply necessary to produce very abundant harvests.

Fages had no soldiers to spare, and Serra and Crespí remained as his

76

uneasy guests. The learned priest and the brash young lieutenant had little in common, and Fages was a man of uncertain temper, jealous of his new authority and ready to quarrel with anyone over mere trifles. As a soldier, he was able and industrious, devoted to the royal service, but he had been pushed ahead by his wife's family connections and had no training in civil affairs or in self-control.

As for Serra, he was waiting impatiently for the arrival of the next vessel so that he could move forward from the standstill at which he found himself. His was the temperament of a man who could write:

> I do not say that everything must be done in one day but I do think that the ship should sail when the wind is favorable.

This far-flung venture had many elements of the quixotic about it—a dream to be achieved with only a handful of men. Two thousand miles removed from the actual scene of operations, Their Excellencies in Mexico City could press for settlements from San Diego to that great bay of San Francisco—"large enough to float all the world's navies"—but be slow to appreciate the enormity of the problems involved. Great myths had surrounded California ever since the sixteenth century, when a novelist had imagined it as an island rich in pearls and gold and ruled by Amazons. Now it had come to seem that the impossible might be achieved. Fortunately, the real California had an eighteenth-century giant—the gray-robed Padre Serra—to spread civilization over more than five hundred miles of coast.

Crespí was complaining of the clammy cold as fogs rolled in from the sea to circle about the wind-twisted cypress trees and settle in his bones. It had been two years since either he or Serra had received a letter "from Christian lands" when the *San Antonio* returned in May of 1771 to give them new encouragement. It brought ten missionaries, ample provisions, and a reinforcement of soldiers.

> Their arrival was the occasion of intense joy to our Venerable Father President, who now saw so many workers who had come burning with zeal to labor in the vineyard of the Lord. By that time the servant of God had built sufficient living quarters to house them, though indeed of palisade construction; they were to live in

these until appointed to cooperate in the labor for the spiritual conquest.

[Palóu]

He appointed two of the missionaries to relieve those in San Diego eager to relinquish this difficult post, and named others in pairs to found four new missions that looked promising on the plans of empire drawn up in Mexico City. Serious obstacles would confront them, but Serra was sanguine. Don Pedro Fages departed southward on the vessel with six of the friars, and with him out of the way, the padre quickly proceeded. He had received official permission to move his headquarters from Monterey to Carmel, and he lost no time in locating a permanent site for the Mission San Carlos Borroméo del Río Carmelo, known also as San Carlos de Monterey.

"WOULD THAT THIS BELL BE HEARD THROUGHOUT THE WORLD!"

That ardent zeal for the conversion of the pagans which glowed

Mission San Carlos de Monterey (Carmel Mission).

Rey Ruppel photos, courtesy Monterey Peninsula Chamber of Co…

in the heart of our Venerable Father Junípero allowed him neither rest nor any delay in putting into effect the practical means for realizing his ambitions. As soon as he finished exploring the area of the Carmel River and left workmen engaging in preparing lumber for building, he returned to Monterey to prepare for his journey into the Sierra of Santa Lucía. He set out with the two fathers assigned as founders of Mission San Antonio. Taking with them all the necessary furnishings for that mission and the requisite military guard, they traveled toward that sierra, twenty-five leagues from Monterey, south-southeast. When they arrived in the heart of that sierra, they came into a large valley which they named the Valley of the Oaks because these trees were abundant. There they pitched camp.

[Palóu]

After months of ascetic self-denial and stalemate, Fray Junípero threw himself passionately into the dedication of the new mission.

Mission of San Antonio de Padua.

Hubert A. Lowman, courtesy California Mission Trails Association, Ltd.

They inspected the terrain and found an extensive and attractive plain in that same valley adjoining a river. . . . They all concurred in the choice of this spot for the settlement; whereupon the Venerable Father ordered the mules to be unloaded and the bells hung from the branch of a tree. As soon as they could be rung, the servant of God began to sound them in a merry peal and to shout as if en-

The burned brick façade of Mission San Antonio de Padua before restoration.

Hubert A. Lou

raptured: "Come, you pagans; come, come to the Holy Church; come, come to receive the Faith of Jesus Christ."

[Palóu]

The two grave priests with him were astonished, and one asked why he rang with such vehemence when not a pagan was to be seen. Serra answered:

"Father, allow my overflowing heart to express itself. Would that this bell be heard throughout the world. . . ."

He was ringing, he said, to fulfill the desires of Sister María de Jesús de Agreda, the seventeenth-century Spanish nun who was reported to have been transported miraculously to pagan lands and prepared the Indians for the reception of Christianity. Stories of the lady in blue, "the flying nun," had been widely circulated throughout the southwest and had a strong influence on the Franciscans.

The bells attracted only one Indian, but soon he was joined by others who brought gifts of wild grains and marveled at the construction of timber houses. They quickly became very much attached to the friars, who gave them glass beads as demonstrations of their love and affection. Satisfied that the beginning of San Antonio de Padua showed unusual promise, Serra departed after a fortnight for Monterey. He had hoped also to found the Mission of San Luis [Obispo de Tolosa] on this journey but could not for lack of troops. He concentrated instead upon the Mission San Carlos, where he lived a sort of hermit life in a little shack.

AMOR A DIOS

. . . There he remained, serving as an overseer and often as an ordinary workman, until a dwelling was completed where he could live and protect himself from the cold wind one feels in that valley almost the year round. The first thing he ordered done was the making of a large cross. This he blessed and raised, with the aid of soldiers and servants, fixing it in the center of the area selected for the mission. This was next to the cabin where he lived and the other cabin which served temporarily in place of a church. . . . As soon as

Interior of Mission San Antonio.

morning dawned, he venerated it while the soldiers sang the *Alabado* [hymn of praise]. . . .

When the pagans came to visit the Venerable Father—and few were the days when they did not come, attracted by curiosity or because of the presents bestowed on them—the first thing he did was to make the Sign of the Cross over them with his own hand, after which he had them venerate the cross. When these sacred ceremonies were finished, he presented them either with food he had prepared for them from cooked wheat or Indian corn, or with a gruel made from these grains, or with glass beads. He tried to please them as much as he could, learning their language by entering into conversation with them.

[Palóu]

He was especially popular with the younger Indians, who called him "The Old Father," as distinguished from the younger Crespí, who had remained at Monterey.

> In their presence he was overjoyed, and he showed them greater affection than if they were his own children. He taught them to greet everyone with the pious phrase: "Love God." This practice was so widely propagated that even the pagans were accustomed to use it, not only when addressing the fathers but also when greeting the Spaniards. The practice became the custom throughout this whole vast region. It softened the hardest heart to hear the pagans, on meeting their fellow Indians or Spaniards along the road, saying those words: "Love God." [*Amor a Dios.*]

[Palóu]

The picturesque missions of California with their beautiful central gardens, shadowed arcades, and stone and adobe walls flaming with bougainvillaea were still far in the future. On this new frontier, they had crude beginnings such as at San Carlos, where a stockade, barely secured at the top because of a shortage of nails, made locking the heavy gate at night a doubtful safeguard. The stockade enclosed primitive buildings whose walls were of mud-plastered timbers and whose leaky flat roofs were of earth. Whitewash covered the interior of the church still to be decorated by the Indians, and Padre Serra's room was a tiny bare cell, furnished only with a bed, a rude table, and a rush stool. Here, as elsewhere during his years as a missionary, he permitted himself no bodily comforts.

> This bed consisted of some roughhewn boards, covered by a blanket serving more as a covering than as an aid to rest, for he never used even a sheepskin covering, such as was customary at our College. Along the road he used to do the same thing. He would stretch the blanket and a pillow on the ground, and he would lie

down on these to get his necessary rest. He always slept with a crucifix upon his breast, in the embrace of his hands. It was about a foot in length. He had carried it with him from the time he was in the novitiate at the College, nor did he ever fail to have it with him.

[Palóu]

At the end of 1771, he was joined at San Carlos by Crespí, and it would be their home mission for the rest of their lives. "The docility and tameness of the Indians" in this region pleased Serra, and he wrote that "although in some parts they are described as somewhat troublesome, it is not a matter of concern. Something must be tolerated for God." And again he wrote, "Although some have declared that these apparently gentle lambs will some day all of them turn into tigers and lions . . . we can say that every day they grow better."

Serra's success in attracting the Indians displeased Fages, who declared that soon they would have too many mouths to feed. The Indians here

The restored kitchen of the padres at Mission San Carlos de Monterey, Carmel.

Hubert A. I

loved the Spaniards, but Fages characterized them as "feeble of spirit" in his *Historical, Political and Natural Description of California.*

> The Indians of this mission and its environs are well proportioned in body, but they do not have the greatest faculties of mind . . . always fearful and unable to retire or make excursions of more than four or five leagues from the port of the Punta de Piños lest they come into conflict with their opponents who resist and persecute them on all sides. They . . . recognize in them [the Spaniards] a shelter and protection of which they were in absolute need. . . .
>
> Only the residents of the village called De los Zanjones, six leagues distant toward San Diego, have been so bold as to attack postriders and travelers, but they have been punished, not without its having cost the lives of a few highway robbers, though they have not been able, thank God, to kill any of our men.

The Indians around San Carlos were attacked by the hill Indians of the Santa Lucía range whenever they went far in search of acorns, and set upon when they cruised the beach above Monterey. Centuries of warfare had made them so timid and apathetic that they did not even make nets or canoes to catch fish, though many of them lived within musketshot of the shore. They existed mostly upon seeds, pine nuts, and berries and underwent great hardships in winter which the padres sought to relieve.

FAMINE

The fathers had only begun to cultivate the land, and all were dependent upon supplies from the ships which, in 1772, were delayed in their once-a-year voyage. Fages lived well, since he had set aside a plentiful store for himself, but his soldiers were half starved, as one of them wrote:

> This sort of thing—working all day without eating—was a common event. And if from time to time we stopped to roll a cigarette he [Fages] let out a flood of oaths—that we were traitors to the King, that we were cheating in our work, that none of us amounted to a row of beans, and that all we thought of was drinking and eating.
>
> Believe it or not, we were in such dire straits that we ate vipers,

rats, snakes, sea skates, coyotes, crows—any animal whatever except the black beetles. And of what grew wild in the fields we ate everything raw which we knew positively would not harm us, worse than so many horses, until most of the men became poisoned. And I was one of the number.

Provisions had not been separately marked for the military and for the missions—another in the growing list of grievances between Serra and Fages—and the padre informed the Viceroy about this starvation period of 1772.

As regards our food supply—to last us a year and to leave something over to give, at least, to the little Christian [Indian] boys and girls—I intended to say a great deal, but will limit myself to this: that our sufferings are great. Never have we, the religious, been in

Detail of Mission San Carlos de Monterey, showing the famous star window and old bell tower.

such dire straits, and never has the said officer been living in such plenty, as since the time he and I arrived in Monterey.

Serra's chief concern was not for himself but for the Indians.

> The greatest sorrow that afflicted the compassionate heart of this servant of God was that he did not have the wherewithal to give the poor Indians what they needed; but he tried to comfort them with kind words, and with his own hands distributed to them food, even that which he himself needed; and he did the same with the few clothes he had. With his own hands he cut out blouses and skirts, as well as shirts and pants for the boys. He became expert in sewing . . . in order to instruct the neophytes. This art they did learn in a short time.
>
> [Palóu]

Hunger afflicted a reconnaissance party, headed by Fages, which returned from a further exploration of San Francisco Bay with Padre Crespí. To relieve its intensity, Fages dashed off on a great bear hunt in the Valley of Los Osos. Serra wished to have a friar accompany him in order to found the Mission of San Luis Obispo nearby, but Fages curtly refused. He would be marching too rapidly to take care of this matter, he said, but Serra took it as another affront and one more of the "vexations, labors, and reverses we have to put up with."

It was coming to seem to him that: "As ever, the worthy gentleman proved, once more, that he had little taste for disposing of affairs that might possibly redound to the credit of the Fathers." The little priest could be sharp-tongued when he chose, and he declared that reinforcements Fages sent out to continue the bear hunt included "the most notorious molesters of gentile women."

STUBBORN CONFLICT

He was of the opinion that Fages cared nothing for the welfare of the Indians, regarded the padres as a nuisance, and wished only to build his own reputation. Both were strong, determined men and neither was inclined to take orders from the other. It was a clash of authority that threatened to wreck the whole precarious venture in New California. The missions could not survive without the military to protect them, and civilization could not take hold without the labors of the missionaries.

Was Fages to be permitted to ride roughshod over the desires of the padres and even to read their mail? Serra's letters had arrived with the seals broken, and he had a suspicion that he had not even received some of them.

In Fages' eyes, Fray Junípero was the impractical dreamer, the fervent mystic ever-seeking to establish more missions with an inadequate guard, relying rather upon the armor of God. Serra, for his part, could point to Fages' inhumane treatment of the soldiers, which was causing them to desert in numbers that were depleting the force as seriously as had the scurvy.

Fages had been in command of the men aboard the ill-fated *San Carlos,* and it was a common saying among the survivors that more had "died of famine than from sickness." Serra was to pass a letter from one of them on to the Viceroy recording that Fages had deprived them of the brandy, vinegar, and freshly killed chickens that could have saved their lives and kept for himself a whole trunk of chocolate. Changes must be made, as Serra was to report to the Viceroy.

> Otherwise there will be no stopping the desertions of the soldiers and others who, up to the present time, have caused so much trouble and will continue to do so. Nor can matters remain as they are, as far as those who stay on are concerned—they stay because they cannot get away. Every one of them is extremely wrought up. Their grievance is not only because of the long hours of work and lack of food . . . but because of the harsh treatment and unbearable manners of the said officer.

Because of desertions and general insubordination among the soldiers, Fray Junípero saw the realization of one of his most cherished projects vanishing into the distance. This was the founding of a mission in the heavily populated region of the Santa Barbara Channel, and it had been one of the first three planned by him and Gálvez. This postponement caused him "deep sorrow," added to his acute anxiety about San Gabriel Arcángel, also known as San Gabriel de los Temblores. Desertions and

Indian hostility had threatened this mission's founding in 1771, but the native leaders had thrown down their bows and arrows at the sight of a painting of Our Lady of Sorrows.

OUTRAGE AT SAN GABRIEL

They were conquered by that beautiful image . . . and the two chiefs rushed forward to place at the feet of the Sovereign Queen the beads they wore around their necks as gifts of their great esteem. Thereby they showed they wanted to be at peace with us. They called together the Indians of the nearby villages whence an ever-growing number of men, women, and children came to see the Most Holy Virgin. . . . The pagans themselves cut and carried the greater part of the lumber for the construction; they helped in building the small houses. . .

When those natives were most happy, one of the soldiers blighted

Mission San Gabriel de los Temblores.

Hubert A. Lowman, courtesy California Mission Trails Association, Ltd.

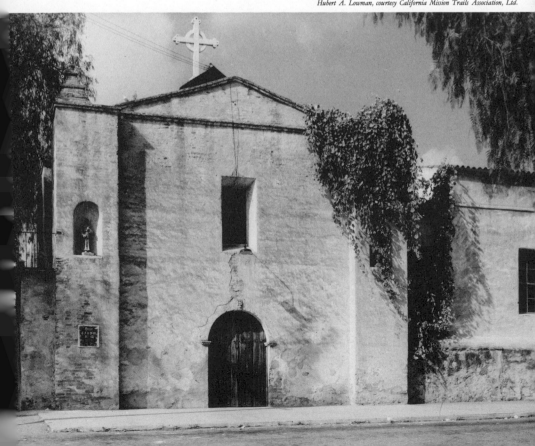

their good will by offending one of the leading chiefs of those villages and (what is even worse) by offending our Lord God. Because both he and his wife were outraged, the chief desired to take revenge. He gathered together the inhabitants of the nearby villages. . . . [and] when the pagans came within musketshot distance, they let loose a volley of arrows, all directed at the soldier who had been the culprit [rapist]. He aimed his musket at the Indian he considered the boldest . . . and killed him. As soon as the rest saw the havoc and realized the power of our men in weapons, they fled hastily, leaving dead the unfortunate chief who had first suffered insult and now death. . . .

Fearing that the pagans would attempt to avenge the death of their chief, he [Fages] determined to increase the guard of Mission San Gabriel to the number of sixteen. For this reason, and because of the little trust he had in the other soldiers because of repeated desertions, the founding of Mission San Buenaventura had to be suspended. . . .

[Palóu]

After these troubles the Indians tended to stay away from the new mission, but distance did not protect them from the soldiers' abuse—as Serra heard from the padres who had founded it. He reported to the Viceroy.

In the morning, six or more soldiers would set out together, with or without permission from the corporal, on horseback, and go to the far distant *rancherías,* even many leagues away. When both men and women at sight of them took to their heels—and this account comes from the Fathers, who learned of it from the many declarations and complaints of the gentiles—the soldiers, clever as they are at lassoing cows and mules, would catch an Indian woman with their lassos to become prey for their unbridled lusts. At times some of the Indian men would try to defend their wives, only to be shot down by bullets. . . .

What with these occurrences and others, a year passed by, not only without making any serious progress, but more and more each

Hubert A. Lowman, courtesy California Mission Trails Association, Ltd.

Outside stairway to choir, Mission San Gabriel.

day turning away the hearts of the gentiles, and pushing them farther away from where their true happiness lay.

Too few mules to carry and distribute provisions even when they arrived . . . too few soldiers to man the garrisons . . . flagrant immorality . . . intense privation and isolation—these were ominous days for New California. The missions were tiny islands surrounded by a sea of problems and thousands of Indians. The flickering light of candles on the altars threatened to be extinguished.

VIII   SERRA AND THE VICEROY
"Right reason and truth are practically the same thing."

Distances were vast and communications so slow that complaints in letters to New Spain took a year for their answers. Serra wrote in August of 1772 to his old friend Fray Rafael Verger, who was now Guardian of San Fernando.

> As regards spiritual matters, much more could be accomplished if we had something to eat, especially, too, if we could remove some obstacles which I will explain later. By them our hands are almost completely tied, and the remedy lies in Mexico. If only one of us could go there and fly back immediately.

When a courier tardily arrived at Monterey with the news that the long-expected supply ships had not been able to make this northern port but had returned to San Diego, Padre Serra determined to make the 450-mile journey southward himself and save the already existing missions from utter collapse. Mules were too scarce to make a huge packtrain to the north, and he would impress the nature of the crisis upon the sea captains. He insisted on accompanying Don Pedro Fages, and en route founded the Mission of San Luis Obispo. Hastening on foot and on muleback as quickly as the rough circuitous trail would permit, he arrived at San Gabriel. His eagerness exalted the small number of converts —one adult and three children—and his vision saw a large future colony herding, tilling, and harvesting on the fertile plain. He reached San Diego in mid-September and immediately went into action.

> Without thinking of taking any rest after so extended a journey

Mission San Luis Obispo de Tolosa.

(which for the servant of God was a painful one because of the habitually diseased condition of his foot and leg), as soon as he arrived he began to confer with the captain in command of the ships, Don Juan Pérez, his countryman. He pointed out to him the impossibility of covering the distance of 170 leagues overland to Monterey. This territory was inhabited all the way by pagans. Moreover, the mules necessary for carrying the cargo were not available, nor were soldiers for guarding the packtrain. He recalled, furthermore, the want that had been suffered because of the delay in the arrival of the ships. This had caused many of the soldiers to desert, and they took refuge among the pagans. . . . He added that if other soldiers had not also deserted, it was only because they hoped that the ship would arrive soon. Now that two ships had arrived, if the soldiers were to experience the same want, they would certainly desert, and from this would certainly result the loss of the three missions already founded in the north.

The Commandant excused himself from sailing up to Monterey on the ground that the season was already far advanced and that winter would catch him precisely at that port where the packet boat would be unable to withstand the storms of that latitude. But the Venerable Father Junípero encouraged him . . . He said the Lord would not permit bad weather if he would perform this service in honor of His Divine Majesty. With these persuasive arguments added to the high opinion he had formed of the virtue of the Venerable Father Junípero, and trusting in his prayers, Commandant Pérez determined to sail his packet boat and its cargo to Monterey, and began immediately to prepare to sail north.

[Palóu]

"FOUR EYES ARE BETTER THAN TWO"

What he heard in San Diego gave Serra further cause for alarm. There were rumors that sailings from San Blas on the mainland were about to be abandoned and that hereafter all supplies would be transported across the gulf and carried overland from Old to New California. Serra could foresee disaster, and he was at rapier-point with Fages over many issues that came to a head in San Diego—the conduct and duties of the soldiers assigned to the missions . . . San Buenaventura . . . the distribution of food, cattle, and mules . . . the location of Indian *rancherías* close to the missions, which Fages considered to be a hazard. Palóu had learned of such conflicts in his letters from Serra, and so he had reported to Verger from Old California.

[Fages] considers himself as absolute and that the missionaries count for less than the least of his soldiers, so that the missionaries cannot speak to him on the slightest matter concerning the missions. He states that he is in charge of all; that the missionaries have nothing more to do than to obey, say Mass, administer the sacraments; that all the rest devolved upon him as commander. . . . If he were a person who understood something about the missions and Indians, one could close an eye [to his actions], but the fact is he understands nothing about such things and is an unbearable character.

95

Another of the missionaries who was in New California with Serra wrote that Fages "has been most domineering in contrast to the patience and suffering of the Father President. It is possible that Fages will write to the governor or to Mexico [the Viceroy] saying that we oppose everything he determines."

In San Diego, Serra learned to his further distress that the two men on whom he had counted most for support in this spiritual conquest—De Croix and Gálvez—had left for Spain. He had always believed that "four eyes are better than two," and in this extremity he sought the advice of the other friars currently living in San Diego. It was clear to them that the new Viceroy could not possibly be acquainted with the problems of New California, and that unless he came to their aid the whole "enterprise will come to naught." One of them must travel to Mexico City and personally state their case to Don Antonio María Bucareli y Ursua, the new Viceroy and an aristocrat with a list of titles as long as his family lineage, which included three popes.

2,000 MILES TO MEXICO CITY

Fray Junípero was the logical choice for this crucial maneuver, which would call for the greatest astuteness and diplomacy, but his health seemed too frail to bear the strain of the journey. He was sixty years old, lame, and suffering also from asthma. After the sea voyage, he would have two hundred leagues to cover on muleback before he reached New Spain's capital, but he refused the offers of others to go in his place. His was a triumph of spirit over an emaciated and worn body when he stepped aboard the *San Carlos* late in October of 1772. With him went an eleven-year-old Indian boy, Juan Evangelista, from San Carlos, as his servant, destined to be perhaps the first cultural-exchange student in history.

Being a good sailor who did not suffer from seasickness, Serra was able to organize the material he was to present to the Viceroy during the fifteen days on the ocean. The urgency of his quest was speeded by what he saw in San Blas, where preparations were being made to dismantle the port. Yet between him and Mexico City stood the specter of death.

When he arrived at the city of Guadalajara . . . both fell prey to a malignant fever [typhoid], so that they were in danger of death and received the Viaticum. The Venerable Father did not feel so badly over his own sickness as he did over that contracted by the Indian, because of what would result at Monterey [if the boy should die]. His relatives and countrymen would never believe his death was due to natural causes. To forestall such grave consequences, he [Serra] besought God in all earnestness (as he later told me on several occasions) for the health of the neophyte, forgetting all about his own. . . . But God willed to restore health to His servant Fray Junípero, as well as to the Indian. As soon as they became halfway well, they continued their journey.

They arrived at the city of Querétaro, forty leagues from Mexico City, where, having been received as a guest at the College of Santa Cruz, the Venerable Father had a recurrence of the same malady. He immediately retired to the infirmary, believing that he would certainly die this time.

[Palóu]

The Indian boy having been saved and his document on the missions sent on ahead, Fray Serra resigned himself to the will of the Lord. If his life's work were over, so be it. He whispered to a visiting doctor who felt his pulse and, turning to an attendant, made a startling diagnosis:

"Is this father going to receive the Last Sacraments? If he is, then I am in a condition to receive them also. Father, get up; you are all right; there is nothing wrong with you" . . . [The superior was called, and the doctor said to him:] "If it were not so late . . . I would have him get up because he is well. But let him get up tomorrow, and after taking food he can continue his journey." This he did, and he arrived at Mexico City on February 6, 1773, very tired, worn, and thin.

So important was the journey of our Venerable Father President to Mexico City that, if he had not undertaken this exhausting trip, the conquest which he had begun would have been in imminent danger of being lost.

[Palóu]

From brush huts to the huge palace of the Viceroy . . . from naked

97

natives to velvet-clad lackeys; the Indian boy was spellbound with wonder. His relatives would scarcely believe what he had to tell, but they would be relieved to know that Spaniards were like other men and had their own women. Nor had they sprung full-grown out of the earth, as some natives thought. Spanish babies cried like Indian babies.

Crouching at the feet of his master, the boy marveled at the curled wig sweeping to the shoulders of the Spanish nobleman, the jewels sparkling on hands that appeared out of cuffs that were crusted with gold. This man could be the God of whom Fray Junípero had told him, and yet from time to time the god took a pinch of snuff. The boy moved closer to the shabby gray tunic of *El Viejo* and was assured by the familiarity of his tonsured head and of the great cross which always hung on his chest. The other man was a strange being, but he had never been afraid of the little padre who was no taller than he.

From time to time Fray Junípero also dipped from a snuffbox while his voice rumbled on through the long afternoon above the sound of wheels in the courtyard large enough to hold one hundred coaches. It seemed to the boy that the Viceroy was listening to the padre intently. The aristocrat of blood was facing an aristocrat of brains and knew that he had much to learn.

THIRTY-TWO POINTS

During a number of such sessions when Serra answered the Viceroy's questions with the incisiveness of an intelligence backed by expert knowledge, he laid down thirty-two points that were likely to determine the fate of New California. If Bucareli could see their merit, they would make the foundations of a workable mission system. If he did not, the missionaries would drift away in discouragement, and it could not survive. The opening points involved emergency measures, and Serra did not mince words.

> I consider it most advisable that the new frigate [on which work had been stopped in San Blas] be got in readiness with the utmost speed possible. . . . I myself have been on board and was amazed at its enormous capacity. One trip with it, added to what the two packet boats can carry, might save from the pangs of famine and starvation both the presidios and the missions—whether already in

being or yet to be founded—and bring content and happiness to the hearts of all. . . .

[Serra]

FAGES MUST GO

Then there was the question of Don Pedro Fages and Serra's request that he be recalled. Though Fages had worked long and conscientiously in his post of duty, he did not care to learn what would make the missions live and instead had stifled them. Serra discussed his grievances with Bucareli verbally and in writing.

> Most excellent Sir, the missions, as is clear from what has been said, are still tender plants and have made little headway because they are as yet new, and also because they lacked the means. Then, too, every step they have made forward, or even hoped to make, has been to the accompaniment of contradictions and obstructions. But, without being at all prejudiced in the matter, I can certainly give Your Excellency the assurance that, on the part of the religious, both as regards the temporal and spiritual progress, no time has been wasted . . . How devotedly the religious have worked and continue to work, God alone knows; but for us that is sufficient.

Serra stated the hard facts about Fages, as he had experienced them, and recommended that Sergeant Don José Francisco Ortega be appointed to the post of commandant. Ortega had been chief scout on Serra's trip to New California with Portolá, and the friar had first-hand knowledge of his bravery and resourcefulness. "The risks he ran in going among so many gentiles [with a single companion] kept me in continual anxiety." Furthermore, Serra had observed that, in contrast with Fages, Ortega's "command of soldiers is firm without rigidity, and has prudence and common sense. I believe they will love him sufficiently without ceasing to fear him."

At the same time, the padre did not wish Fages to be hurt by disgrace. It was Serra's nature to be forgiving, and he implored: "I beg and beseech Your Excellency that he may be discharged honorably and without any humiliation whatsoever; and I pray God to bless him."

Bucareli, too, had a keen mind and was a sharp judge of men. Serra was making a mighty impression upon him. He could readily see that this was not a man who would bow before any throne or make any shallow concession for the sake of peace. The Viceroy was aware that he could find other military commanders, while Serra would be irreplaceable. The missionaries alone had the stamina and the profound faith that enabled them to endure the loneliness and hardships of that far frontier and, under Serra's leadership, to nourish "tender plants" that might flourish into colonies. Spain must hold its grip upon New California.

This remarkable priest was as thorough in presenting his demands as any chief executive in the field of business, though his hope for gain was not money but the saving of souls. Fray Junípero had a rare gift for organization and putting a finger upon the stumbling blocks. It must have crossed the Viceroy's mind that here was a man who could have been rich had he not turned to the priesthood and taken the vow of poverty.

Scores of pages addressed to Bucareli in March of 1773 left no detail untouched. Serra's superior at San Fernando had requested that he make such a document of the thirty-two points. In turn the padre asked the Viceroy to send him copies of all future orders. Both sets could stand "for the record."

Serra's petitions were well considered and sound. He provided information that called attention also to fraud. The scales at San Blas cheated the weights; corn was sent out riddled by grubs; the meat crawled with maggots. His document named the number of guards and mules essential to each of the missions . . . asked that stores and letters for the religious and for the military be separately marked . . . insisted that any soldier of scandalous conduct be removed from any mission at the request of the resident padres.

The military commander should be notified that the "training, governance, punishment, and education of baptized Indians . . . belong exclusively to the Missionary Fathers [a serious point of friction], the only exception being for capital offenses. . . . This is an essential condition for the rightful training of the poor neophytes." The contrary had prevailed, which had resulted in "the worst of evils."

The Viceroy read on through the well-formed handwriting that called attention to each phase of their conversations. It was a document that would give him a firm basis for clarifying the troubled situation before the Junta, the executive body of New Spain's government. Bucareli was convinced that the purse strings must be loosened and the friars given a stronger voice.

Serra asked for more bells, vestments, and holy images . . . pointed out the urgent need for blacksmiths, forges, and carpenters . . . asked that the stock herds be given to the care of the padres. "There is every chance that we will take better care of the animals then they do at the presidio. This will also give us the chance to get a little more milk to help our little Christians—this being almost the only food we have been able to give them thus far." He finished by asking pardon for all the soldiers who had deserted in order "to give peace of mind to the gentiles and regain these poor culprits."

> To sum up: Your Excellency . . . will graciously decide, order, and command whatever may seem most fitting to you. . . . My wishes are that you will arrive at these decisions as soon as possible, so that I may be able the sooner to take to the road once more to return to that poverty-stricken and far-distant vineyard of the Lord. And seeing that the present state of my health is none too good, I will have to make that trip somewhat slowly. . . .
>
> Most Excellent Sir
>
> Kissing the hand of Your Excellency,
>
> Your most humble servant and chaplain, who holds you in the highest respect, etc.,
>
> > Fray Junípero Serra

1,500 MULES

Serra was still in Mexico City in April, and, though Bucareli had already granted many of his requests, a major threat still remained. He summed it up in a research report to the Viceroy so comprehensive in scope that it would demolish all contrary arguments. It was incredible what he had learned about mules!

> It has come to my attention that a number of people are proposing to lay before Your Excellency's Higher Authority a plan to abandon the town of San Blas and the line of navigation from that port to San Diego and Monterey. To date, this line has been maintained

for the upkeep of the new missions and the royal presidio there. They wish, by so doing, to curtail the enormous outlay of money that both of these occasion to the royal treasury; and they would make good the loss of the two—I am referring to San Blas and the merchant ships—by sending overland from Loreto or San Fernando de Velicatá, by means of an adequate number of mules and their mule drivers, the amount of supplies which heretofore has been carried by the afore-mentioned ships. It seems opportune that I should express my opinion on the matter, and I do so by summing up the situation as follows:

1. To transport the above-mentioned supplies by land is not only fraught with the utmost difficulty, but it is morally impossible.
2. Even though this method were adopted, and pushed with might and main, it would be far more expensive than the method we are at present employing.
3. That if we adopted the plan we would most assuredly lose our brightest prospects, which are the very fine qualities favoring spiritual conquest of this entire area.

And now for my arguments to back up these statements. . . .

[Old California had been largely stripped of mules; they would have to be brought across the Gulf of California from the mainland.] Let us consider how large a number of mules would be required to make the plan in any way feasible. . . . One item is for 150 loads of flour, and these would need as many mules. . . .

Likewise: The two boats last year carried 800 fanegas of corn [a fanega was about 1.6 bushels]; to transport a like amount by land would require the services of 400 mules. . . .

Likewise: As regards the consignments of chocolate, clothes, and other articles . . . it would call for at least 100 mules.

Likewise: As regards groceries that are usually sent . . . beans, lentils, peas, rice, meat, butter, biscuits, sugar, greens, besides vinegar for scurvy, soap, tobacco, etc.; again it seems to me that anything less than 150 mules could not handle the job.

Likewise: As regards the muleteers required . . . my opinion is it would take no less than 100 men. . . . The mule drivers, going on horseback as they usually do, will have to have as many saddle horses and their harness.

Then there is this to consider: Just as the sailors, besides what they carry to the ports as cargo, also set aside their own provisions of food for seven or eight months for the round trip, so with the muleteers and their [soldier] escorts . . . The transportation of provisions for so many men for such a length of time would require—in my opinion—not less than 200 mules.

Besides what has been said, one might ask of those experienced in such matters, as regards the 1,100 mules and their bulging baggage which we have thus far counted—and likely enough we are far below requirements—how many will be needed for replacements in a trip of more than 500 leagues, and on roads which are most of the time rough? How many saddle mules, and how many pack mules would have to be replaced? Just as a guess—and I am probably too low . . . I put it at 400. . . .

I leave out of count the extra mules needed to pack the kitchen utensils, and the bags and trappings of the mule drivers; and the mules needed if some artisans, families, laborers, etc. go along.

But restricting ourselves to what we have counted, I put the question:

When can we expect shiploads in Loreto of mules, assembled and shipped from the opposite coast [across the Gulf of California], to the number of 1,500—our figure up to the present? How is it that today, after three years spent on the job, they have put their hands on so few? . . .

But granting that all goes well, how are we to feed so large a number of animals in [Old] California during the time they are herded together and preparations are being made for their loading and equipment? . . .

Serra pointed out further that the outlay of money at San Blas had not been due so much to the cost of sailings to Monterey as to the building of new ships and warehouses. If the mule-train idea were adopted, would these expensive structures now be burned? He had been told that the ships would be used to transport mules and supplies across the Gulf of Loreto, so where would be the saving in sailors? Fray Junípero could build up formidable opposition when he was aroused. A realist, he reserved his gentleness for the Indians. Piety alone would not protect the missions.

SEARCHING ARGUMENTS

Another question: What will be the market price of the 1,500 mules we have figured just now? What commission will the dealers make who are to buy them, and keep them till they can be put on board ship? And the cost of their complete outfitting—sweat blankets, pack saddles, saddle blankets, etc.—quite an item when you are putting 1,100 mules on the road! . . . To all of these questions, I do not suggest any answer myself, seeing that it is an easy matter for Your Excellency to get information from anybody in the packtrain business . . . Only one thing will I say: beyond any doubt whatever, the cost will be faraway greater [than sea transportation].

The third point—of no less importance than the preceding two— needs no more proof than is provided each day by the soldiers who, without any fear of God whatever in their hearts, give such scandal in those far distant parts. Your Excellency has been fully informed about it.

The continual passage of packtrains, one following the other, for a distance of more than three hundred leagues through gentile country; the presence of so many mule drivers—men, for the most part, from the dregs of society, bereft of high principles and conscience— will not all this occasion the utmost disgust and aversion: will it not be the cause of quarrels and disputes with the poor downtrodden gentiles? . . . .

Then, too, the presence of so many women there—it would be a great miracle, yes, a whole series of miracles, if it did not provoke so many men of such low character to disorders which we have to lament in all our missions. They occur every day; it is as though a plague of immorality had broken out. . . .

To all of this there must be added the curiosity and vivacity of the gentiles themselves, especially those living in the Santa Barbara Channel, who want to see everything; and when they get the opportunity of stealing, especially iron, they will not miss it. Now to our men this has been a cause for killing, as has happened many a time. .... On my last trip from Monterey to San Diego, in one of the towns along the Channel, notwithstanding my presence and remonstrances, a man was killed and another left dying. . .

The passing to and fro of so many packtrains will cause, Most Excellent Sir, the continuation and reception of such evils which must be considered as unavoidable. It is certain that the poor gentiles, until now as gentle as sheep, will turn on us like tigers. They will make it impossible for our couriers to pass through their land; and their good will toward us will be lost. . . . Their peaceful and quiet disposition of mind is a factor which leads them to accept the most sweet law of the Holy Gospel. . . . They have received the religious and the soldiers with the greatest demonstrations of happiness and joy.

Padre Serra had stated his case. Adoption of the new overland plan would be no economy and would mean a great setback if not destruction to the scheme of empire in New California.

IX   DISASTER AT SAN DIEGO
"Some who have gone away would gladly take what they left."

Don Antonio María Bucareli y Ursua, the elegant Spanish grandee and alter ego of King Carlos III, proved to be a stanch friend at court. He had received Fray Junípero with utmost cordiality and interest and was to provide him with the strong backing that would give fresh vitality to the California conquest. For his part, Serra gave equal assurance in the course of a letter written to the palace in May of 1773.

> I may further add this: if Your Excellency will kindly order proper measures to be taken—as indeed you are now doing—and remove hindrances, I take the future as witness that before long, with the help of God, the outlook will be totally changed. That certainty, together with the longing I am bound to entertain to see such vast countries incorporated into the fold of our Holy Mother Church, and subjected to the Crown of our Catholic and most pious Monarch, whom God keep, has been the one and only reason of my laborious journey here. This I consider more each day as time well spent, since I have experienced so many favors from Your Excellency.

During his stay in Mexico City, Serra also wrote one of his rare personal letters addressed to his nephew, who had become a Capuchin monk. His warmly human emotions and intense self-discipline are clearly revealed.

> My not answering the various letters I have received from Your Reverence was not due to any lack of affection for you. When I left my country which was so dear to me, I made up my mind to leave it

not merely in body alone. With many people I could have kept up friendly relationships by letter. . . . I have many acquaintances and friends both inside and outside the Order. But if I were continually to keep before my mind what I had left behind, of what use would it be to leave at all? . . . . Although I know I am a sorry sort of person— useless and unworthy—every day during the Holy Sacrifice of the Mass, most especially, do I commend to God my one and only and dearest sister Juana, your mother, and her children, and in particular my Capuchin. It gives me pleasure to think that all of you do the same for me, so that the Lord may be at my side as I move amidst dangers from naked and barbarous men. . . . Once again I am ready to make my way to that far-off vineyard of the Lord.

In the mission field to which I am returning, only once a year is there an opportunity to receive letters from this College or write to it. And, if right here they get only one letter from us throughout the year, what wonder is it if we are slow in writing to other parts of the world?

As Fray Junípero told his nephew, he hoped to spend the rest of his life in the mission field. Hearing that he was about to be elected Guardian of San Fernando College, he fled from this signal honor to the port of San Blas long before his ship was due to depart. An administrative office indoors, a desk job, had no appeal for him. The challenge lay in the risks and relentless activity of New California. As one of his colleagues noted, he consistently showed "the qualities of a lion whom only fever could lay low."

Sailing was delayed so that he did not reach San Diego until March of 1774, bringing with him a doctor, carpenters, blacksmiths, and laborers. He had been gone for nearly a year and a half, and the success of his interviews with Bucareli increased his delight at being back in the land of the Indians.

New California had almost succumbed to famine during his absence, and the Spaniards around Monterey had survived largely on herbs and milk without bread or any other item of food. However, Fray Junípero had arrived on the new frigate which, with its enormous capacity, "would banish cruel hunger from the settlements once and for all." Without his timely protests, the *Santiago* would have been burned for salvage of the scrap iron.

JUAN BAUTISTA DE ANZA

This was only one of the results of his visit to Bucareli, and others were to follow with startling frequency. On his road northward that spring, he encountered a remarkable figure with deep-set brooding eyes, magnificent mustachios, and hair that swept to his shoulders. This was Juan Bautista de Anza, the famous frontier fighter. A new route of communication from the mainland of Mexico (not the peninsula of Old California) had been opened to strengthen the slender threads that held New California together.

Bucareli had discussed this possibility with Serra—whether it would be desirable to come up from Sonora—and Serra's optimism had swung the balance. Now Fray Junípero could look forward to seeing a whole line of colonists, cattle, and mules following Anza along the trail from northern Mexico to Monterey across the deserts of the Southwest. Another builder of empire was on the move!

Bucareli had ordered this first land expedition of Anza's, but he did not stop there.

> Because of the frequent meetings and lengthy conversations which His Excellency had with the fervent Fray Junípero during the seven months he remained in Mexico City, he [Bucareli] became deeply imbued with a religious zeal for the conversion of souls and the extension of our Holy Catholic Faith and the dominions of our King. This zeal animated him in such a manner that there was no slaking the thirst for souls which the continuous discussion with the Venerable Father on this delightful matter of converting the pagans caused him. . . . He disclosed . . . his desire to send a maritime expedition [farther north up the coast] . . . to discover if it was inhabited and if there might be a port around which to found new missions. . .
>
> On hearing this, the Venerable Father Junípero—who was insatiable in these matters, and whose thirst was never quenched when it came to extending the boundaries of Christendom, and who never

considered any difficulty that might be placed in his way—not only praised the idea but tried to aid him in executing it. He told the Viceroy that with the frigate [*Santiago*] he had ordered completed, and with Captain Don Juan Pérez, His Excellency had exactly what he needed to carry out that enterprise, for the frigate could sail from Monterey as soon as it had unloaded the cargo of foodstuffs and supplies. Such was the impression which His Excellency had formed of the Venerable Fray Junípero that, without further consultation than the opinion given by His Reverence, he issued the corresponding orders for the expedition.

[Palóu]

PERILOUS VOYAGE

A more worldly pen might add that politics and foreign affairs had a strong influence on these decisions of Bucareli's. Spain had not lost its fear that the Russians were about to sweep down the coast.

To fulfill the pious desires and the good intention of His Excellency, the Venerable Father sent along two missionaries, Fray Juan Crespí and Fray Tomás de la Peña Saravia, who gladly sacrificed themselves for a voyage so perilous as the surveying of an unknown and uncharted coast. Because it was neither known nor charted, they would be in continuous danger of running aground on some island, shoal, or rocks, and being shipwrecked without possibility of rescue. . . . After receiving the blessing of their superior, they embarked on June 11, 1774, and on that day the frigate sailed. It returned, casting anchor at Monterey on August 27, meeting no other misfortune than that a few of the crew contracted scurvy.

By means of this survey, at least part of His Excellency's desires were carried out, for the frigate sailed as far north as 55°. There they found a large island which projects far into the sea, which they named Santa Margarita [northern tip of Queen Charlotte's Island off the coast of Canada]. . . . They noted that the entire coast was peopled with pagans [who came out in canoes] although the navigators did not land anywhere. [They attempted this at Vancouver Island but encountered a violent storm.]

[Palóu]

A second daring sea expedition was to follow in the spring of 1775 and another in 1779. To the sailors, these voyages into unknown waters held almost the same terrors as those experienced by the crews of Columbus. Palóu gave them copious coverage.

> Even though the Venerable Father President Fray Junípero did not participate personally in these sea expeditions, I could not but insert accounts of them . . . since they were brought about by his difficult journey to Mexico and aided by the influence of his apostolic zeal on the noble and religious heart of His Excellency. They were directed to the extension of the Catholic faith to the most remote regions. The Viceroy was confident that this primary object of these expeditions would be obtained through the indefatigable zeal of the Venerable Father Junípero.

"CRUEL HUNGER BANISHED"

Serra's faith was as boundless as the glorious prospects he saw for New California, which he expressed in a letter to the Viceroy shortly after his return.

> After so many journeys by sea and land, I am here well and safe in the missions of Monterey, so greatly favored by Your Excellency. Now all the land, heretofore so melancholy and miserable, is rejoicing because of the abundant provisions and most fitting measures with which your Excellency has consoled us. . . .

To Bucareli's secretary he wrote further:

> Now all of a sudden we see ourselves supplied with such abundance that we do not know where to store all the victuals. The rations have been increased. The pay has been raised. [Serra had not received even the humblest priest's stipend until he reported this oversight to the Viceroy.] And relieved from anxiety, all the people are in the greatest mood for rejoicing.

He declared that "All past sufferings are turned to joy" and that "All the inhabitants are so happy and so contented that there is no trace of sadness except in those who have to leave." He painted an idyllic picture for the Viceroy.

> Just to see a hundred boys and girls of about the same size, to hear them pray and answer questions [the number baptized at San Carlos now numbered two hundred and forty-five, many of them children under eight] . . . to hear them sing, to see them all dressed in worsted clothes and woolens; to see how happy they are at play, and how they run up to the Father, as if they had known him all their lives. . . .
>
> From *rancherías* very far distant and lost in the folds of the mountains they arrive every day. . . . They see the church and how nice it looks; they see the corn fields, which appear wonderful in their eyes. They see the throngs of children and all the rest of the people, how they are clothed and sing and eat in plenty, even though they have to work.

Serra was too much of a realist not to admit that it was chiefly food and fabric which enticed them as they surrounded him on the road crying out "Love God, Father! Hail Jesus!" With wry humor he added that this was often followed by "Chuqui! Chuqui!", a request for tobacco.

To add to his pleasure, Palóu had joined him to await another assignment. The Dominicans had taken over the missions of Old California, and the prophecy of the two friends had been fulfilled: "We will meet in Monterey!"

The new regulations issued as a result of his trip to Mexico City granted nearly all of Serra's requests, except that Ortega be appointed as commandant. The post had gone to Don Fernando de Rivera y Moncada, middle-aged captain of dragoons. Rivera was popular with the soldiers but had no reputation for either imagination or audacity. Ortega had been passed over because he was only a sergeant. Serra had misgivings about Rivera, and he was disturbed over the crestfallen Fages, who was about to depart. Perhaps he had been too harsh in his criticism, and in a letter to the Viceroy he gallantly sought to make amends.

Since my arrival back at this mission, I have noticed, on the part of this gentleman [Fages], much politeness and quite a degree of self-consciousness. It has caused me much distress. . .

By God's great goodness, never did I aim to do him any harm. . . . I acted only because I felt it my bounden duty to work for his removal which, as far as I could judge, was necessary for the prosperity of the country and the relief of its inhabitants. . . . He declares that . . . the mistakes he made originated not from malice, but from sheer lack of understanding and reflection.

I have lived among soldiers, have faced the same dangers as they . . . I have done all that it was in my power to do. Therefore, Most Excellent Lord, if these, my loyal services, amount to anything in the eyes of the army authorities, I grant and relinquish all, and surrender it . . . in favor and in behalf of Don Pedro Fages. He has no knowledge of what I am doing . . . I am acting entirely of my own accord. . . .

I seek for no publicity. Of what moment is it for the world to know that this worthless friar has been of some small service to the Crown? Let the whole credit go to Don Pedro Fages.

The harvests were good that year of 1774. The Indians caught barrels of sardines, and Serra, strolling down the beach to watch them around their fires, found it "as good as seeing a theatrical show." Juan Evangelista, the little Indian boy "who amused Your Excellency so," was sending his regal patron a keg of dried fish as a special gift and telling his people of the fabulous sights he had seen: the Spaniards were so rich that Mexico City glittered with gold and jewels . . . they had their choice of beautiful women in satins and lace. The older men of the tribe listened and nodded their heads. It must be true what the padres had told them—that the Spaniards had come among them, not to rob but only to work for their happiness.

"Now certainly we believe you," they said to Serra.

Hereafter, what could impede progress in New California? Friars and food were on hand to supply the four new missions that Bucareli was urging as a result of his conversations with Fray Junípero. Serra wrote him with a clear and farsighted view.

In looking over the sweep of our conquests, I am quite convinced we should found the four missions we have spoken about. If placed at proper intervals—say every twenty-five leagues. . . . they would form from San Diego to here [Monterey] stepping stones, so that every third day one might sleep in a village. With that peace would be assured, and passage through the country made easy.

RELUCTANT RIVERA

Still Rivera made excuses and took no action. He dragged his boots, was vacillating and timid. In January of 1775, Serra voiced his protests in a letter to the Viceroy. He declared that, of the five missions that had already gained a toehold, some had never had good military protection and yet had experienced only friendliness from the Indians, as in the case of San Antonio. The presidio at Monterey was jammed with soldiers . . . friars were fretting to be sent to new posts . . . and still Rivera evaded the issue.

When I hear that there is no possibility of sparing seven or eight men and a few animals to found a mission . . . Your Excellency may well imagine how it disturbs me. That military men should move forward with caution is well and good; but for the kingdom of God some boldness is more in keeping that all these cautions they are forever urging on me.

[Serra]

In defense Rivera was claiming:

These Fathers of San Fernando have their minds filled with nothing but increasing the number of their missions. This must be done, come what may, without the necessary number of soldiers and without any prudence . . . and without keeping in mind that Indians are always Indians. And so the whole enterprise runs a risk of being a total loss.

Bucareli regarded Serra as a saint, but he could not grant him such power as to arouse suspicion of the clergy and their motives and alienate the military arm of the government. Thus he was also coming to recognize that Fray Junípero could be a troublesome kind of saint, prickly and tough-minded. Serra admitted this freely when the current Guardian of San Fernando advised him to be more moderate.

> And as to what Your Reverence adds—that in all other matters that may come up I should try to preserve good relations with the said officer [Rivera]—I will not say that I have done so, or do so, in everything, since I am full of faults. I will only say that I wanted peace, and I will try to keep peace, with the help of God.
>
> They tell me that he [Rivera] is asking persistently to be removed, and I fear they may grant it. I consider it better that this one should tire little by little of disagreements than that another should come with new vigor, since we must consider it a regular occurrence that disagreements will not be lacking, more or less.
>
> [Serra]

Annoyed at Rivera's persistent procrastination, Serra pointed out later that concentrating soldiers within a presidio instead of employing them to guard new missions was no safeguard. Of what use were soldiers who could sleep soundly through an Indian attack? One new mission had barely been dedicated at San Juan Capistrano—the first in three years— when tragedy struck elsewhere.

"A CRUEL RESOLVE TO KILL THEM"

> During the month of November of the year 1775, Venerable Father Lector Fray Luis Jayme . . . and Father Preacher Fray Vicente Fuster . . . were administering Mission San Diego with great joy of soul . . . The mission constituted a populous town. . . .
>
> Whilst the fathers and the new Christians [sixty recently baptized during the Feast of St. Francis] were so happily and comfortably situated, the fury of the chief enemy of souls [Satan] increased . . . To carry out his diabolical aims, he made use of two neophytes of the group baptized earlier. These . . . left the mission and traveled through the villages of the sierra. He incited those Indians to spread the report among the pagans . . . that the fathers wanted to uproot paganism entirely and forcibly make Christians of them all. . . . All who heard this were thrown into confusion—some believing it, others doubting it. . . . But the greater number believed the state-

ment . . . So when the enemy found them favorably disposed, he incited in them a passionate anger against the Fathers, which begot a cruel resolve to kill them as well as the soldiers who guarded them and to set fire to the mission and thus destroy everything.

Some groups invited others to participate, yet some towns held off, the natives declaring that the Fathers had done them no harm, nor did they force anyone to become a Christian. . . .

More than a thousand Indians gathered together. . . . They agreed to separate into two bodies, one to fall upon the mission, the other upon the presidio. The latter group . . . was to set fire to the presidio and kill the soldiers as soon as they saw the mission in flames. . . .

They arrived in the valley of the San Diego River on the night of November 4. There they separated. Half of them, assigned to attack the presidio, marched toward it [five or six miles away]. The others, without being detected, approached the huts where the neophytes lived at the mission . . . to prevent anyone from escaping [under threat of death] or giving the alarm. . . . The greater number of them went to the church and sacristy to rob clothing, church goods, and whatever else they could find. Others with fire brands which they found in the barracks of the soldiers—of whom there were only three and a corporal, and evidently they were asleep—began to set fire to the barracks and all the rooms. As a result of this and the terrifying cries of the pagans, all awoke.

MARTYRED FRIAR

The soldiers sprang to arms while the Indians were already shooting their arrows. The priests were sleeping in separate rooms. . . . Father Fray Luis . . . on hearing the noise of the shouts and the crackling of the fire, came out and, seeing a great number of Indians, approached them, greeting them in the accustomed manner: "Love God, my sons." The Indians . . . as wolves do to a young lamb, laid hold of him . . . They conducted him through the thickets of the arroyo, where they divested him of his holy habit. In his naked state, they began to strike the Venerable Father with their clubs and shot countless arrows through his body. Their furious anger was not satiated with taking his life with such great cruelty, for after he was dead they beat his face, head, and the rest of his body so that from head to foot there remained not a sound portion of him except his consecrated hands. . . .

The blacksmith was about to go outside with sword in hand, but . . . the Indians released a terrible volley of arrows and killed him. When the mission carpenter saw this, he seized a loaded rifle, fired, and shot down one of the pagans who were near the door. . . . The other carpenter from the presidio . . . who was sick in bed, was also shot with arrows and fatally wounded. . . .

The largest group of pagans was engaged in fighting the soldiers who were in the hut that served as their barracks. Here were also Father Fray Vicente Fuster, two small boys [son and nephew of the lieutenant in command of the presidio], and the carpenter who was not wounded.

[Palóu]

Seeing the mission in flames, the Indians who had intended to attack the presidio returned to join the frenzied mob and celebrate the death of Fray Jayme with a barbarous dance. The presidio and the mission were visible from each other, and the Indians assumed that the soldiers would rush to its aid. As it turned out, not a soldier there stirred from his bed, since none was on guard. They neither saw the blaze nor were aroused by the gun fire.

The small group of soldiers at the mission was able to defend itself against such a multitude of pagans with great bravery. . . . When the enemies saw their strong resistance and the casualties which our soldiers inflicted, they set fire to . . . the palings [surrounding the barracks]. In order not to be burned alive, our men came out bravely and took their positions in a little adobe room, the kitchen. For protection that structure had only three adobe walls. . . . Its roof consisted merely of some branches which the cook had placed there to protect himself from the sun. After our men took refuge in this kitchen, they showered continuous volleys of shots and defended themselves against the great crowd who harried them exceedingly from the unwalled side of the room, through which they shot arrows and hurled clubs.

[Palóu]

Two of the soldiers were wounded and put out of action when they dared to rush out to one of the burning buildings and stagger back with bundles and boxes to build a fourth wall. For defense against hundreds of Indians, there remained only the corporal, one soldier, and the carpenter. The corporal, a good marksman, ordered the others to load and prime the guns while he did the shooting, killing or wounding every Indian who showed himself. The savages then set fire to the branches above the heads of the beleaguered Spaniards, causing fear that the sparks might fall into the gunpowder.

This would have happened had not the foresight of Father Fray Vicente caused him to cover the powder sack with the skirts of his habit, not minding the danger to which he himself was exposed. When the Indians saw that the fire on the roof did not cause the soldiers to come out, they tried to force them out by throwing lighted brands and pieces of adobe within. One of these latter struck the priest . . . although he did not suffer serious consequences.

Thus they kept on fighting until dawn, the beautiful light of which forced the pagans to flee in the fear that soldiers from the presidio would come. They went away, carrying with them their dead and wounded. . . .

When it dawned on that November 5, and after the great multitude of pagans had disappeared, the neophytes came out of their little houses and went immediately to see the father who was in the kitchen-fort with the corporal and three soldiers, all wounded. The corporal, though wounded, did not want to say so lest the rest lose courage. He [Fuster] asked them about Father Luis, about whom he had worried all night . . . The soldiers tried to cheer him by saying that he had gone to hide in the willows. . . .

The Indians found the Venerable Father Fray Luis dead in the arroyo and so disfigured that they hardly recognized him. . . . When Father Fray Vicente beheld this sight, he was beside himself until the wailing of the neophytes who so heartily loved their deceased father made him break into tears.

[Palóu]

Mission San Diego, the first to be established, lay in ruins, and the soldiers of the presidio belatedly thirsted for revenge.

X CROSS FIRES

"I do think the ship should sail when the wind is favorable."

"Blood of the martyrs" . . . this thought of heroic death for the Faith had stirred Fray Junípero ever since early youth when he had read the lives of the saints. Mystical ecstasy was his first reaction to the tragic news from San Diego, borne hundreds of miles through mountain passes and rain-flooded arroyos by soldier-couriers. Palóu heard him say:

> "Thanks be to God, now indeed the land has been watered [with blood]. Certainly now the conversion of the Indians of San Diego will be achieved."

Rivera prepared to leave Monterey at once for the south, while Indian neophytes and soldiers from the presidio gathered to attend the solemn requiem for the slain padre. Indians of the whole region had been aroused, and rumors ran that all the missions might be attacked. Ignoring these perils, Serra pleaded with Rivera to let him join his party, but the commandant refused. A lame priest on muleback would be only a hindrance.

Except for Fray Junípero, those at the Monterey presidio and at the Carmel mission were in a state of panic. His ardor was kindled at the prospect of becoming himself a bloody sacrifice.

ALARM AT SAN CARLOS

> The news was spread about among the neophyte Indians that the wild tribe, named the Zanjones, who lived about six leagues from Mission San Carlos, intended to destroy the mission, just as had the pagans of San Diego. Although full credence was not given to this report, care was taken to have the soldiers in readiness. . .

In a few days there came an Indian neophyte woman, thoroughly frightened and full of fear. With great weeping, she told the corporal that the Zanjones were already coming down the valley . . . very numerous and well armed. . . . [Serra informed the five other priests who were there with him, including Palóu and Crespí.] He was full of joy—for apparently he believed for certain that that night they would take his life. . . .

When we came out of the church [after making confession one to another], we met . . . the soldiers of the presidio who were preparing for the defense of the mission, for it was already night. . . . [Their leader] suggested that it would be better if we all slept in one room, so that we could defend ourselves. It was a little room of adobe with a tile roof which served as a forge for the blacksmith. Thus we would be well protected against arrows and fire. . . . [Serra] did not let us sleep all night because his abounding joy did not allow him to stop talking. He recounted many similar situations in order to give us courage. And in the morning not a single Indian of the Zanjones was to be seen. We concluded from that that either the heavy downpour of rain that fell that night prevented them from coming, or the whole thing was an imaginary tale of the Indian woman, induced by the fear they have of that warlike tribe. But the fright and fear were great for all, except for the servant of God, whose joy was without measure.

[Palóu]

Father Fray Luis Jayme had died a "blessed death," in Serra's view, and his chief concern now was that the rebellious Indians who had led the attack be shown mercy. It was ironic, he wrote to the Viceroy, that after all had been destroyed, the military forces were coming together "to set things aright" by rounding up the ringleaders for punishment. Spanish cruelty would drive the natives away and undo all the work of the missions.

Most Excellent Lord, one of the most important requests I made [of Gálvez] . . . at the beginning of these conquests was: if ever the Indians, whether they be gentiles or Christian, killed me they should be forgiven. The same request I make of Your Excellency [in the present case]. . . .

119

While the missionary is alive, let the soldiers guard him and watch over him, like the pupils of God's very eyes. That is as it should be. Nor do I disdain such favor for myself. But after the missionary has been killed, what can be gained by campaigns?

Some will say to frighten them and prevent them from killing others.

What I say is that, in order to prevent them from killing others, keep better guard over them than they did over the one who was killed. As to the murderer, let him live, in order that he should be saved—which is the very purpose of our coming here and the reason which justifies it. Give him to understand, after a moderate amount of punishment, that he is being pardoned in accordance with our [Christian] law which commands us to forgive injuries. Let us prepare him, not for death but for eternal life.

"BLOODLESS MARTYRDOM"

Again the ecclesiastical mind and the military mind were in conflict. Bucareli came to agree with Serra, but in the long interval before he could expect a reply, the friar suffered deep mental anguish. Interminable delays and great distances and doubt as to the course of events in the south made the spring of 1776 for him "a prolonged and bloodless martyrdom." The friars with him at San Carlos, who had waited nearly two years to be sent out to new missions, were growing restive, and the future of the whole enterprise lay under heavy clouds. Not that the padres were idle, as Serra wrote to the Viceroy.

[They] have been constantly in the fields: one with the men, another with the women, a third with the children, a fourth in the garden; in short, all of them fully occupied, not to mention prayers three times a day. . . . Such work in the fields seems alien to our holy vocation, but it has the same end in view. . . . But the more abundant our crops gathered are, the more numerous are the consumers. . . . We have three hundred and more mouths to feed without counting the religious and the household servants. . . The fact is even yet we cannot give them food as it should be prepared for want of cauldrons to cook it in. . . . [Even so, it was not so difficult to feed the neophytes as to cover their nakedness, an outward sign of their conversion.] Today at this hour there is almost nothing to be found [neither blankets nor cloth], and when I look at my audience in church I can scarcely see anything else than animal pelts.

What was happening on the other side of the continent—the struggle of the American colonies against England—was a world away from the western wilderness where the tolling of the mission bells could be stilled any hour. Apprehension of a general uprising among the Indians was now acute, an aggravation of the danger that had always existed. Again and again, Serra tried to impress the Viceroy with the need for more soldiers to guard the missions.

> In front of them, behind them, to the right and to the left of them, they are surrounded by an immense gentile population . . . If any of the Fathers has to attend to anything at any distance and needs an escort of two soldiers, there are only two left at home. When any other job has to be attended to . . . to go and wash clothes, to go after a cow that is missing, to go hunting or something of that kind, we are left without any soldier. And yet, almost every day a great number of gentiles, sometimes more than fifty in a body, comes either to pay us a visit or to bring a present or make some request. Up to now we have not been able to supply sufficient Christianized Indians for our defense, since most of those baptized are children.
>
> [Serra]

At the time of the San Diego disaster, there were only eighty soldiers in New California, but Anza arrived in time to help Rivera capture the worst of the culprits. With the sudden pressures put upon him and his resources, the commandant was half distracted. To add to his woes, Anza was riding at the head of his second expedition under orders to found a presidio and mission that Rivera had done his utmost to discourage. This was the much-discussed settlement at the Port of San Francisco. Rivera was reluctant to extend the area of his responsibilities, and he had reported that his explorations had revealed no suitable site.

Now he was confronted with a bold and resolute leader at the head of a hungry and impoverished horde of colonists in a trek from Mexico that marked a milestone in pioneer history. With the skill and audacity which Rivera lacked, Anza had been able to bring two hundred and forty men, women, and children and over a thousand cattle, horses, and mules some sixteen hundred miles from the mainland of Mexico. Though they had traveled through flood and storm, and eight babies had been born on the way, not a single human life had been lost. It was a record that has seldom been equaled.

Rivera became surly when Anza refused to remain and help him protect San Diego. The dangers there were exaggerated, Anza felt, and he could delay no longer in his march northward to execute the command of the Viceroy. If Rivera refused to cooperate, that was his business.

Anza found no hospitable reception at Monterey, and even Fray Junípero's welcome was mixed with consternation. How would they ever manage to feed such a crowd? Monterey was poorly equipped to take care of them, as Padre Pedro Font, Anza's chaplain, recorded.

> It is all a small affair, and for lack of houses the people live in great discomfort. The commander [Anza] indeed had to lodge in the storehouse, and I am in a dirty little room full of lime while the rest of the people accommodate themselves in the plaza with their tents as best they could.

Writing to the Guardian of San Fernando from Carmel, Serra gave a distressed account of the situation.

> Seeing that Don Fernando [Rivera] did not leave [San Diego], nor give him [Anza] the key to his room, and seeing that there was nobody there to give him a bite to eat or a cup of chocolate . . . he came here with his lieutenant . . . and a whole flock of others. . . On March 22, they left here for San Francisco [to explore it for themselves] and on April 8 returned here once more.
>
> As soon as he got back he wrote to Don Fernando that he would wait for him about twenty-five days. But on getting no answer during that time [by courier] he has already gone back; and his people,

seeing that they are not going where they expected, are far from satisfied.

Of those who have been added to our numbers, there are more than 200. If the boat be delayed, and an attack is made on the provisions of the missions, it will be pitiful, especially here where we have been facing the prospect of a bad harvest, since this year [winter] we have had less rain than any time since we have been here.

Don Bautista de Anza is apparently much displeased at the dilatoriness and lack of initiative on the part of Don Fernando. Who knows if they understand one another?

Anza had given the charge of the colonists over to Lieutenant Commander Joseph Moraga, and his departure from Monterey marked a touching scene between the leader and the poor homesick people who, for nearly a year, had looked to him as their source of strength. Usually reticent, Anza also gave way to emotion, as he wrote:

This day has been the saddest one experienced by the presidio since its founding. When I mounted my horse in the plaza, the people whom I have led from their fatherland, to which I am returning . . . most of them, especially of the female sex, came to me sobbing with tears which they declared they were shedding more because of my departure than of their exile, filling me with compassion. They showered me with embraces, best wishes, and praises which I do not merit. But in remembrance of them . . . and the affection I have for them ever since I recruited them, and in eulogy of their faithfulness, for up to now we have not seen a single sign of desertion . . . I may be permitted to record this praise of a people who, as time goes on, will be very useful to the monarchy in whose service they have voluntarily left their relatives and their fatherland which is all they have to lose.

Anza started on his way south with nineteen packs of baggage, which included some unwilling passengers, as Font remarked:

In a cage we carried cats, two for San Gabriel and two for San Diego, at the request of the fathers who urgently asked for them,

123

since they are very welcome on account of the great abundance of mice.

FURIOUS ENCOUNTER

They were not far distant from Monterey when they met a weird figure on muleback. It was Rivera, muffled to the eyes in serapes and wild with rage at sight of Anza. All expected that they would be turning back to Monterey for a conference, but Rivera rode angrily past.

> He and I embraced, but the two captains saluted each other very stiffly, for the venomous spirit of Señor Rivera was patent at once. They spoke very few words, and these impulsively, and then, leaving Señor Anza with his words in his mouth, as they say, Señor Rivera said to him, "Adios, adios." Then spurring on his mule, he hurried on his way, so red in the face, so choleric, and so irritated with everybody that he did not say goodbye to anybody else except Anza, and in the way I have related.
>
> [Font]

It was not only his jealousy of Anza that was causing Rivera to act like a madman. Tempers had risen to such heat in San Diego that he had been excommunicated by Padre Fuster, and he was riding north to tell his version of the episode to Fray Junípero. Rivera's offense had been to invade the chapel where the rebel chief Carlos had taken refuge and to remove him forcibly in defiance of church sanctuary.

Goaded by Anza, who had rebuked him sharply by letter, saying that further delay over San Francisco would arouse the Viceroy's anger, Rivera was literally beside himself. He got little satisfaction from Serra, who was desperate to get to San Diego himself, and retaliated by denying him military escort. Yet he no longer dared block Lieutenant Moraga in his progress to San Francisco. With the arrival of two packet boats in June with provisions, some members of Moraga's party were to go by sea and others by land.

BIRTH OF SAN FRANCISCO

> The Venerable Father President decided that we two missionaries [Palóu and Fray Pedro Cambón] should go with the land expe-

124

dition ... It comprised Lieutenant Commander Don Joseph Moraga, a sergeant, and sixteen leather-jacket soldiers, all married men, with the large families also of seven married colonists, together with the families of some dependents and servants of these settlers, cowherds and muleteers who led the cattle from the presidio, and the packtrain with foodstuffs. . . . [They arrived in the neighborhood of the Port after a ten-day journey.]

A camp was formed, composed of fifteen field tents, by the side of a large lagoon emptying into the arm of the sea of the port ... The purpose of the encampment was to await the arrival of the ship [*San Carlos*] to determine the site of the presidio on the basis of the anchorage place. As soon as the expedition came to a standstill, many pagans arrived, all peaceful, showing signs of joy at our arrival and even more so when they saw that we treated them kindly and gave them little gifts, both beads and our kinds of food, to attract them. They repeated their visits, bringing gifts of their poor resources which comprised clams and grass seeds. . . .

When we saw that the ship was tardy in arriving, we decided to begin to cut wood for the construction of the presidio near the entrance of the port, and for the building of the mission on this same site of the lagoon [Laguna de los Dolores] in the plain toward the west. When it was realized that we had been there a month, and that neither the ship nor an order from Commander Rivera had come [for the founding of mission and presidio] nor were the soldiers sent [the mission was to have twelve as a guard], the Lieutenant decided to leave us six soldiers . . . as well as two colonists. With all the rest of the people he transferred to a place near the entrance to the port [in the vicinity of the Golden Gate] in order to begin work [on the presidio]. . . .

[Palóu]

This was the site where Font had stood beside Anza marveling at this "harbor of harbors," and watching "the spouting of whales, a shoal of dolphins or tunny fish, sea otter and sea lions."

The packet boat entered the port on August 18, having been delayed by contrary winds which forced it south [below San Diego]. . .

With the aid of the sailors . . . a building was put up at the presidio to serve as a chapel and another as a warehouse for the storage of foodstuffs. At the mission another building was constructed for the chapel, and still another with its compartments for the living quarters of the priests. The soldiers built their houses both at the presidio and at the mission out of wood, with a roof of tule [rushes].

On the feast of the Imprinting of the Stigmata of Our Seraphic Father St. Francis, patron of the presidio and port, September 17 [1776], the solemn taking possession of the presidio occurred. On that day I sang the first Mass, after the holy cross had been blessed, venerated, and set up . . . amid many a cannon volley from land and sea and fusillades by the soldiers.

[Palóu]

One of the great cities of the Western world was to grow out of these

Mission San Francisco de Asís (Mission Dolores).

Hubert A. Lowman, courtesy California Mission Trails Associatio

pioneer exertions made in the same year the Declaration of Independence was signed on the eastern seaboard.

Since it was time for the packet boat to return to San Blas, and since no order from Commandant Rivera had come to found the Mission of San Francisco, Our Father, they decided to take possession and inaugurate it [after further extensive exploration of the magnificent bay and the river that emptied into it]. This was done on October 9.

The site was blessed, the holy cross set up, and a procession was held with the statue of Our Father St. Francis carried on a platform and later placed on the altar. . . . At the founding, the people of the presidio, of the ship, and of the mission assisted, the soldiers firing volleys during all the ceremonies.

[Palóu]

Interior of Mission San Francisco de Asís.

Hubert A. Lowman

Meanwhile Serra had been able to arrange transportation to San Diego. His relations with mariners had always been more amicable than with the military, and he boarded the *San Antonio*. Rivera had returned to San Diego, where sight of Serra filled him with trepidation. He was convinced that the padre was on his way to Mexico City, again to voice his complaints.

> As soon as we anchored [at San Diego], Fathers Lasuén and Murrio came on board in the company of Don Fernando [Rivera]. This gentleman's countenance, as the officers of the boat noticed, was pale with apprehension because of my arrival. I did not notice it at all. But once he was back at the presidio with the said Fathers, he went to bed, saying that he was sick. To Father Lasuén, who went to pay him a visit, he confided that he was all upset . . . and that he had made up his mind he should put on the girdle of Our Father Saint Francis and begin a new life, etc.
>
> [Serra to his Guardian]

Once Serra had talked with the three missionaries living there—the two from San Juan Capistrano and the one who had survived the San Diego tragedy—he went to the heart of the matter.

> After they had been consoled and encouraged by him, they stated that their greatest trial was to see nothing being done and themselves unoccupied. . . . [The Indians were again peaceful.]
>
> With his great patience and abundant prudence, he [Serra] waited until the vessel had discharged its cargo. When this work was about finished, he spoke to the ship's commander, Don Diego Choquet, asking if the sailors could come and help to work on [rebuilding] the mission. . . . Like a gentleman, he [Choquet] replied that it would be a great pleasure, and that not only the sailors would work, but he himself also, as an ordinary laborer. . . .
>
> All the sailors were armed with swords and guns, prepared for any eventuality. All the Indian neophytes capable of working, and the corporal with the five soldiers went along. Upon their arrival at the site [five or six miles from the presidio], the work was divided among the men, who amounted to fifty ordinary laborers, in addition to

ranch hands and cooks. Some began to carry stones, others to lay foundations, still others to make adobe bricks . . . not only the pilot and boatswain . . . but also the priests and the captain of the packet boat served as overseers.

The work went forward with such intensity, and the men labored with such enthusiasm that, on the basis of what they had done in two weeks, they felt they certainly would finish the construction, enclosed by an adobe wall, before the sailing of the ship [in mid-October].

[Palóu]

SHAME AT SAN DIEGO

At this point, Rivera stepped on the scene to interfere. Under the circumstances, he had been unable to refuse Serra a small guard, but now he took alarm at a report from some of the Indian neophytes. They repeated the rumor that the Indians were about to strike for a second time. Taking the ship's captain aside, Rivera advised him and his crew to return to their vessel. Unwilling to face the friars himself, he asked Choquet to notify them, saying, "I will not tell them, as I know they will feel bad about it."

The captain of the ship, despite all his earnestness, reasoning, and personal persuasiveness, could not budge him from his stand. He asked him if he had made any attempts to find out the truth of the matter. Rivera said he had not; but from the mere fact the Indians were repeating the rumor, doubtless it was true.

The naval captain then replied: "Well, Sir, on a former occasion when a similar rumor was current before we came here to begin this work, you ordered an investigation made through the sergeant, and the rumor was found to be false. All the villages were in great peace, all the Indians very contrite and repentant. Why not investigate now? With so many armed men here, there is nothing to fear. To me it seems more to the point that, if there exists a genuine reason to fear, the guard be increased with more troops rather than be called away, to the discredit of the arms of Spain." All these reasons, instead of convincing him, made him more stubborn; and, giving the strict order for the troops to retire, he marched off to the presidio.

The captain of the ship conveyed to the Fathers the news of the order given by the military commandant. . . . He told them: "I can see no reason for the retreat. The action is a matter of great shame. But I do not want to have quarrels with this man, and so I have decided that we should leave here."

[Palóu]

To Choquet, as to Serra, the whole thing was senseless.

The Fathers felt this keenly, the Venerable Father President most of all. As soon as he saw that all had retired, he was almost beside himself. He was at a loss to put the sorrow of his heart into words except to say: "Let the will of God be done. He alone can bring us help. . . ."

Each measure taken by the commandant of these establishments which impeded or retarded the conversion of the pagans was to the Father President an arrow sharper than those which took away the life of the Venerable Father Fray Luis Jayme. . . . Seeing that he had no human recourse, he turned to God for help as the Lord of the vineyard . . . charging the priests to do the same.

[Palóu]

As was his custom in times of duress, Serra kept nightlong vigils, resting only at the time of siesta. The soldiers on guard always heard him praying, and they were wont to say: "We do not know when Father Junípero sleeps."

XI ECHO OF CHANGE

"Which is the more trying position: to have the appetite to eat and have no food, or have plenty to eat and no appetite?"

As though in answer to Serra's prayers, a reinforcement of twenty-five soldiers arrived from Old California in late September, three weeks after the labors at San Diego had been suspended. Rivera could no longer use excuses and rumors as a shield for his fears. He appointed an adequate guard to assist in rebuilding Mission San Diego, assigned others to found San Juan Capistrano for the second time, and added two leather-jackets for the protection of San Gabriel.

Satisfied that the burned-out mission would rise again, Fray Junípero prepared to leave for San Juan Capistrano to dig up the mission bells, which had been buried for safety. From there he traveled fifty miles to San Gabriel, undertaking the taxing journey in order to bring back cattle, foodstuffs, and neophytes to help in constructing the new mission in a fertile valley set amidst rolling hills within sound of the sea. He was so eager to return that he scoffed at possible hazard and went on ahead of the packtrain with only one soldier and one neophyte.

MORTAL RISK

About midway on the journey . . . he realized that he was in evident danger of death at the hands of the pagans. . . . A large crowd . . . came out upon them on the road, all painted and well armed, their arrows in readiness to kill the priest and the soldier, with the purpose no doubt of obtaining the cattle. God delivered them by means of the neophyte who . . . yelled out to them not to kill the father, for many soldiers were following and these would kill them.

Mission San Juan Capistrano.

Hearing this in their own language and dialect, they desisted. The priest called to them, and they approached him, now transformed into gentle lambs. He blessed them all, as was ever his custom, and then gave them beads as presents. . . [Having won their friendship] he continued on his way without further incident except for the fatigue of the journey and the pain in his foot. . . .

With the aid of the interpreter . . . brought along from San Gabriel, he lost no time in telling the pagans that the principal purpose which induced the fathers to come hither and live among them was to teach them the way to heaven. . . They understood this so readily, and were so impressed by the statement, that they soon began to ask for baptism. The result was that . . . just as pagans of other missions had been a nuisance in asking the fathers for food and other small

Mission garden of San Juan Capistrano.

Hubert A. Lowman, California Mission Trails Association

Mission San Juan Capistrano.

gifts, those of San Juan Capistrano were a nuisance in asking for baptism [and impatient that they must wait for instruction].

[Palóu]

Here at Capistrano, as at the other missions, the Indians were enthralled by the beauty of the church furnishings and pageantry. The Fathers might be living in rude, miserable huts, but the House of the Lord must be richly adorned. These Spaniards, far from all the other niceties of civilization, set their wilderness altars with the choicest of sacred vessels and candelabra made by the silver workers of Mexico, and donned magnificent chasubles of white, red, or purple from the looms of Europe and the Far East.

From their shabby workaday tunics, they emerged as celestial messengers before the awestruck eyes of the Indians. An Indian who had worn a baptismal cap of Brittany linen trimmed with ribbons and lace was set apart from his fellows, and soon might be taught to sing hymns and chants. These were illuminated on great leaves of parchment with the notes painted in different colors to indicate tenor and bass.

Each time a new mission was started, Fray Junípero strove to give the church some resemblance to a cathedral. It was a demand made not only by the deep spirituality of the Spaniards but also by their knowledge of how to appeal to the Indians. Serra and other missionaries were keen students of psychology from years of experience. They knew how readily the natives could be stirred by colorful ceremonies and statues of saints; a religious canvas could have a profound effect, as in an incident at San Diego. Here, at the sight of a painting, Indian women had crowded around the stockade and thrust their breasts through the palings to offer suck to "that tender and beautiful child" held in the arms of the Virgin.

The wide acceptance of Christianity among the California Indians was also due in part to the fact that they had no clear conception of a Supreme Being, though they had cult-religions that were often complex. Palóu wrote:

> Thus they have not found the least difficulty in accepting any of our beliefs. Some superstitions and vain observances only have been found among them. Among the old people, some have idle tales, such as that they can make it rain, cause acorns to grow, etc., that they can cause the whales or schools of fish to come down, and so on.

But these people [sorcerers and medicine men] are easily proved to be deceivers and are marked and considered as such by the natives themselves, because they make these claims for the sake of the gifts they may receive.

As Padre Serra took to the trail for the long journey back to Monterey, seemingly tireless despite his age and bodily frailties, he could begin to see a pattern of life emerging along *El Camino Real* at the scattered missions he visited. Font described it in his diary.

MISSION LIFE

The method which the Fathers observed in the reductions [conversions] is not to oblige anyone to become a Christian, admitting only those who voluntarily offer themselves. This they do in the following manner: Since these Indians are accustomed to live in the fields and hills like the beasts, the Fathers require that if they be Christians they shall no longer go to the forest, but must live at the mission. If they leave the *ranchería,* as they call the little villages of huts and homes of the Indians, they will go to seek them and will punish them [using the lash or the stocks]. With this they begin to catechize the heathen who voluntarily come, teaching them to make the sign of the cross and other things necessary. If they persevere in the catechism for two or three months and in the same frame of mind when they are instructed, they proceed to baptize them.

The routine for every day is as follows: In the morning at sunrise Mass is regularly said; and at it . . . assemble all the Indians. The Father recites to all of them the Christian doctrine, concluding with the *Alabado,* which is sung at all the missions and in the same key.
. . . . Then they go to eat their breakfast of *atole* [corn-meal porridge] which is given to everybody, making the sign of the cross and saying the *Bendito* before eating it. [The bells rang each change of the day.] Afterward they go to work at whatever they can do, the fathers encouraging them and teaching them to labor by their own example. At noon they eat their *pozole* [thick soup of meat, wheat, and corn] which is made in community for all, and then they work for another spell [four or five hours a day]. At sunset they again recite the doctrine and conclude by singing the *Alabado.*

Mission Bell at San Carlos de Monterey, Carmel.

Because of the great variety of Indian dialects in the community, it was difficult to transfer padres from one mission to another. Efforts were made to teach the Indians to speak Castilian, but only the brightest among the adults could master another language. It was the children who became the linguists.

> The Christians are distinguished from the heathen in that an effort is made to have them go somewhat clothed or covered. . . If any Indian wishes to go to the mountains to see his relatives or hunt acorns, they give him permission for a specified number of days. As a rule they do not fail to return, and sometimes they come bringing some heathen relatives who remain for the catechism, either through the example of others or attracted by the *pozole,* which they like better than their herbs and foods of the mountains. And so these Indians are usually caught by the mouth.
>
> In the missions an effort is made to have the large unmarried girls sleep apart in some privacy. At the mission of San Luis I saw that a married soldier served as mayordomo [superintendent] of the mission, thus giving the Fathers some relief. His wife looked after the unmarried girls. In the daytime she kept them with her teaching them to sew and other things. At night she locked them in a room where she had them secure against insult [seduction by Indian braves or leather-jackets], and for this reason they are called nuns.
>
> [Font]

In their efforts to civilize the Indians, the padres were teaching them the routine of work to replace their old way of life and also making inroads upon habits that, to the friars, seemed unduly promiscuous. What Palóu wrote about the natives around San Francisco was the general case everywhere in New California.

POLYGAMY

> Their marriages have no other ceremony than mutual agreement, and they last until there is a quarrel, when they separate. Then they marry another man or woman, the children generally going with the mother. The only expression they use concerning the dissolution of a marriage is: "I threw her over," or "I threw him over." Neverthe-

less, many married couples, both young and old, have been found who live together quite harmoniously and enjoy great peace, and where the parents and children evince a mutual love.

The bond of affinity is no bar to their marriages; rather, it inclines them to take to wife their sisters-in-law, and even their mothers-in-law. The custom they observe is that when a man takes a wife, he also takes all her sisters. He has many wives but this does not result in . . . even the slightest jealousy, since the second and third wife looks upon her sister's children with the same love as her own, while all live in the same house.

[Palóu]

Naturally, the padres were opposed to this practice of polygamy and urged the marriage of one husband to one wife in a permanent union according to Roman doctrine. They were angered at the immorality rampant among the soldiers, but encouraged their lawful marriage to Indian girls. Serra had requested of the Viceroy that such soldiers be given a bounty of land and livestock and be allowed to remain at the wife's mission.

WEARY MILES

So the mission bells greeting Fray Junípero rang the echo of change along *El Camino Real*. With his bare feet thrust in sandals and his dark eyes reflective under the flat wide-brimmed hat, he jogged northward at mule-pace. His meal was a bit of bread or a tortilla, the ground his bed. The small spare figure with the gray tunic whipping about him in the cold wind was determined to found the mission at San Francisco if it had not yet been achieved. He had been away from San Carlos six months, and news was slow to travel. He had been able to accomplish nothing as yet about the Channel missions, and it saddened him, as he wrote to Bucareli about one phase of this rough journey.

In this, my third and most recent journey along the Santa Barbara Channel . . . we met with high winds, downpours of rain, and much mud. Because the seas were lashed by storms and running high, we could not walk along the beach. . . [This] would have meant a great saving to us, both in the length and quality of our excursions [but] these poor gentiles acquired a new title for our consideration. They have waited so long for the blessings which have been so much delayed for them. . . . Tears welled up into my eyes when I saw with what good will they came to my assistance, linking me on both sides by the arm to get me over the muddy steep hills which I could not negotiate either on foot or on horseback. It was sad to think I would not be able—nor do I know when I will be enabled—to repay them as I would for all their sympathy and trouble.

What a pleasure it was for me to see them, in great numbers, walking along the road with me, and breaking out into song each time I started a tune for them to take up. When the first batch took its leave, a second group . . . would come up for me to make the sign of the cross on their foreheads. Some followed me many days.

By January of 1777, Serra was back at San Carlos to hear stirring news. The settlement at San Francisco had been accomplished and was shortly to be followed by another at Santa Clara, also in the Bay area, bringing the total number of missions to eight. And there were other bulletins even more startling.

MONTEREY MADE THE CAPITAL

Out of touch with developments, he had not been aware of the reverberations from Mexico City as a result of the Viceroy's anger at the timidity of Rivera. Once the ship captain had informed him of the "shame to Spanish arms" at San Diego, Bucareli acted quickly in the name of the king. He needed a strong man as military leader and administrator in New California.

Rivera was to be transferred to Old California, now much the lesser province of Spanish conquest. Governor Felipe de Neve was already on his way from Loreto, and Monterey was to be the capital of both Californias. Serra expressed his reactions to the Viceroy.

The pleasure which I have experienced, and still feel, at seeing our own Monterey, whose birth I witnessed, now made the capital of so large a province, and that the King, our lord, should choose so distinguished an officer [Neve] in charge, is hard for me to describe. I am perfectly aware that this gentleman has made a deep impression— and rightly so—on Your Excellency. As far as I am concerned, he captured my fancy while he was still in [Old] California. . . .

I have begun to . . . promise myself . . . how much help may be expected from his sense of fairness, his prudent way of acting, the energy he puts into all he does, and from all his other good qualities which Your Excellency mentions, in favor of the missions that are already established as well as for a number of new ones. . . .

I will spend myself to the last ounce of my strength, so that I may better help in forwarding his plans for the good of religion. I am under the impression that, in zeal and desire . . . to spread this Christianity, and in being in a position to formulate plans . . . he has many advantages over me.

GOVERNOR NEVE

Don Felipe de Neve was a member of an old noble family with political influence in Spain and Mexico; Serra had learned of him in letters and by reputation. He was aware also that some in high places were insisting that the friars must not be allowed to gain too much power and needed to be kept in their place. No matter—Serra also was astute and skilled at maneuver; he would stand his ground. He was determined to concentrate upon what he felt to be right—the protection of the Indians and the conversion of souls for the glory of God. The wanton shooting of Indians on other frontiers and cheating them of their lands would have appalled him.

It was obvious to Serra that the Crown placed great trust in Neve. After several conferences. he could report to the current Guardian of his College, Fray Francisco Pangua, that Neve was determined to make the authorities open their purse strings. On his journey north, Neve had seen for himself how poor the missions were and "would not be satisfied with anything small."

In fine, I am no soothsayer, but I have conceived the highest hopes that we will live in peace, which has been, and is, my greatest longing. I am in hopes of having to deal with a gentleman, who shows himself to be such by his education—one who can give an answer to what is put before him, and can pay proper attention to what you tell him. On my part, I firmly resolve . . . to work in complete harmony with him.

[Serra]

Neve moved into Spain's newest capital homesick for his family in Seville, whom he had not seen in more than a decade. He had frequently tried to resign. Font had described the forlornness and deficiencies of Monterey where Neve proceeded to strengthen the presidio:

> The buildings form a square, on one side of which is the house of the commander and the storehouse in which the storekeeper lives. On the opposite side are a little chapel and the quarters or barracks of the soldiers, and on the other side are some huts or small houses of the families and people who live there. All are built of logs and mud, with some adobe; and the square or plaza of the presidio, which is not large, is enclosed by a stockade or wall of logs.

Though no foreign power had been seen off this coast, despite Spanish apprehensions, Neve had strict orders not to permit the bold maritime explorer from England, Captain James Cook, to land under any circumstances. Cook was on his third voyage of discovery, which took him as far north as Bering Strait and later to his death (1779) in the Sandwich Islands. As for Fray Junípero, he plunged into a strenuous round of activity among the Indians, doing the work that lay closest to hand.

> Whenever he returned to it [San Carlos], it seemed to him, after having seen the others, that he was the laziest and most slothful of all the missionaries, for he used to say: "I return edified by what the others have done and what I have seen accomplished at the other missions. Here we are always behind."

> [Palóu]

MISSIONS DISJOINTED

Driving himself ceaselessly, Serra deplored the hours he had to spend at the writing desk corresponding with the other missions and with Mexico City. The years were closing in on him, and he felt that his time was short. It was not until fall that he was able to visit the new missions to the north and have long talks with Palóu. What distressed him most was the fact that the line of missions was still so disjointed that the line of communication north and south could be readily cut by the Indians, especially along the Channel.

The greatest danger comes from the heedless action of the soldiers, which cause them [the Indians] to revolt. . . Anyway . . . the danger is always there, and each time we pass through the midst of such a large gentile population, without meeting some act of hostility, can be considered, if not miraculous, at least as a very special providence of God.

[Serra]

Though a Channel mission had been one of the first projects for New California, he had been unable to impress the military commanders with the need to give it top priority.

By taking this simple line of action, couriers from Monterey to San Diego could sleep every night in Christian pueblos, and in places that are well defended. In this way, it would not be necessary to expose their tired animals to the whims of the gentiles, with every chance of losing them, nor would they be constantly exposed to an outbreak on the part of the said gentiles during their repeated journeyings. . . Without such precautions, I feel very much afraid in regard to the constant passing to and fro of our men through that ill-omened, yet fascinating, Santa Barbara Channel.

[Serra]

Serra hoped that, with Neve, such a mission might be the first order of business, but again he was disappointed. The governor turned his forces in other directions, and it would be five years before another mission was built in a start at solving the hazardous Channel problem. Again Serra was frustrated in his dream of casting "the apostolic net" to convert all the Indians along over five hundred miles of coast.

CALIFORNIA'S FIRST TOWN

The Founding of a Town of Spaniards, under the title of
San Joseph de Guadalupe

In order to encourage and stabilize this spiritual conquest, His Excellency the Viceroy charged the new governor, Don Felipe Neve, to make an attempt to settle the land with some towns of Spaniards, who were to be employed in agriculture and stock raising, and in this way aid in the development of these new establishments. Calling this superior order to mind, and having seen (when he came to visit this royal presidio and port [of San Francisco]) the great plains on which Mission Santa Clara is located, and the great amount of land that could be irrigated from the abundant waters of the River Nuestra Señora de Guadalupe, that gentleman brought together the people who had come in the expedition from Sonora [with Anza]. He added others to these, assigning a site and parceling out the lands to form a town [present-day San Jose]. . . . He assigned a place above Mission Santa Clara . . . about three-quarters of a league away from the houses of the mission.

At that site the colonists laid out their town, inaugurating it during the first days of November, 1777. Other settlers have joined these. All are governed by an *alcalde* [mayor] from among the settlers themselves. . . . All go to hear Mass at the mission. They support themselves from the harvests of wheat, corn, and beans which they gather; what is left over they sell to the soldiers, and with the proceeds they buy clothing. For the same purpose they raise cattle and sheep, and also mares to provide the soldiers with horses, etc.

[Palóu]

Fray Junípero saw a threat to the missions in the establishment of a pueblo, which might spread vice among the Indians. He tolerated the presidios and the soldiers—all too often drawn from the scum of society— only because they were a necessary evil, but the trend of events now caused him alarm. Liquor, gambling, and prostitution would follow in the wake of the pueblos. Serra regarded the Indians as the mischievous but lovable children of the religious and knew how easily most human beings could be tempted and corrupted.

Serra believed that it was the missions which could make the country prosper, and he had discussed this at length with Governor Neve. Early that summer they had talked about bringing in more livestock and cultivating vineyards and orchards. Serra had been convinced that Neve would go about this "with his usual efficiency," and so he had reported to the Viceroy. It was a letter that revealed two strikingly diverse sides of his

Hubert A. Lowman, courtesy California Mission Trails Association, Ltd.

Mission Santa Clara de Asís.

nature—poetic ecstasy and stern practicality. (Bucareli had informed him that he was having a silver monstrance made for San Francisco, and it was of this that Serra spoke.)

John H. Livingstone,
courtesy Harry Downie, Carmel Mission

Serra's silver monstrance.

And so, Most Excellent Lord, when Our Most Divine Lord will be placed in it [the monstrance], and a procession shall wind its way over the surrounding fields, the breezes that blow will dance their happiness, and give outward testimony to heaven and earth that our Christian Faith and religion have reached that far-distant boundary.

He continued with an account of the urgent need for blacksmiths and carpenters, especially since two had been killed at San Diego. Monterey could not send artisans to make doors and hinges for the rebuilt mission because it was already so overpressed with demands that other missions often had to wait for a year to get their plowshares and axes repaired. Also "some masons, potters, and brickmakers would be very useful."

Although Neve and other promoters of pueblos might call Serra other-worldly, he had always made it clear to Bucareli that his feet were firmly fixed on solid earth.

XII   LIKE A GENERAL

"The fact is that troubles abound everywhere, a little more here, a little less there."

With a power shift in New Spain, the missions were soon to lose their best ally and friend, and Serra would be dealing with a much younger and less seasoned man than Bucareli. The Interior Provinces, including the Californias, were transferred by the king from the jurisdiction of the Viceroy to Don Teodoro de Croix, nephew of the man who had rejoiced at the raising of flag and cross at Monterey. Henceforth, Bucareli would be responsible only for providing them with supplies, and in June of 1778 Serra was writing to him out of a heart filled equally with sadness and gratitude. Typically, he took no credit to himself for the great strides made since his crucial journey to Mexico City.

> When I realized that this new disposition of affairs was to divert all that marvelous stream of blessings and kindnesses which had ever flowed from Your Excellency at my unworthy asking for the betterment of these poor souls up here, my heart was indeed heavy within me. . . .
>
> When Your Excellency first started your term of office—a period of unparalleled progress—the establishments up north here counted no more than a single presidio and four missions. The missions, and the presidio as well, were in a decidedly formative and delicate condition. . . .
>
> There was not at that time a single mission that could boast of having harvested a grain of any seed. As for food, even we, the religious, had our hard times . . . everything was as a thing very much in its beginnings.

Your Excellency took the enterprise in hand and now the presidios number three with storehouses full of provisions, and supplies have never failed.

The missions are eight in number. Baptisms performed in the first four of them alone some time ago passed the two thousand mark; and baptisms performed in the four which Your Excellency counts to your credit . . . have exceeded six hundred. All of these missions, with the exception of San Diego, maintain all the Christians they have. Over and above, two of the missions have supplied several hundred fanegas [about 1.6 bushels] to the royal warehouse in exchange for cloth to cover the Indians who harvested the crops. In addition the missions have helped one another whenever their needs required it. . . .

Only on the subject of pueblos of Spaniards, and the way they have begun to establish them, have I in private conversations expressed my opinion that it did not appear to me the best thing to do. . . Even the purpose they claimed for the pueblos—that they would thereby have people who would fill the royal warehouses with provisions and so . . . would not depend on the arrival of the boats—such a purpose would be better obtained by increasing and helping the Missions than by means of such pueblos. . . By helping them, they would also be aiding their spiritual advancement. And thus that is the way they will find it to be.

The position I upheld was that the settlers who can suitably fit into such a scheme—and at present their numbers are few—should be distributed until more promising times among the missions.

He pointed out how much wiser it would have been to put Spanish energies into establishing a mission midway along the Santa Barbara Channel and settling farmers around it than to have cornfields within stone's throw of the cow corrals of Santa Clara, but concluded:

To sum up: everything is so different, Most Excellent Lord, from what it was when Your Excellency began to govern, that there is the same difference between both as between real life and a poor painting.

To the formal ending, Serra added a fervent salutation: "Your most devoted servant and chaplain, who reveres and loves you greatly."

The missions were far more than centers devoted to religious instruction. They served also as frontier trade and agricultural schools, transforming natives into farmers, cattlemen, and artisans. Indians were shown the value of work and its rewards in terms of food, clothing, and harvest. Tanneries, carpenter shops, and smithies sprang up around the missions, while red tiles to replace the original roofs of mud and rushes were fired in kilns. The tiles were hand-shaped on wooden forms and not upon the thighs of the Indians, as some later-day guides spun the tale. After Indians set fire to the thatch of San Luis Obispo with blazing arrows, the use of tiles spread throughout the whole mission chain.

Tiles were fashioned originally by the ingenuity of one of the many friars who developed amazing skills to meet worldly demands. Craftsmen and laborers from Mexico were few and scattered in these early days, and it was largely the padres who engineered irrigation systems to water their fields. Some were called upon to teach the women to weave blankets and coarse cloth from wool, and others to contrive wine presses and threshing floors.

Despite all the obstacles and privations, the missions could already show such a record of progress that Fray Junípero could see no place for pueblos until some future time. Were all his heroic struggles to put them on a sound working basis to prove in vain? Funds diverted to the pueblos would weaken the missions and their endeavors to turn the Indians into useful subjects of the Crown, and he stated the case to De Croix in forthright terms.

"MISSIONS, MY LORD, MISSIONS"!

I have thought over the new plan—to set up among these gentiles pueblos composed of Spaniards, or of people of mixed blood, instead of increasing the number of missions. But I have never been able to see or recognize any advantage in it whatever, either on the temporal or spiritual side. Quite the contrary, it appeared to me to have many drawbacks.

The governor knows what I think on this matter. . .

Let these pueblos be established, well and good, if the authorities approve of the plan; and let the missions disappear. But I want it to be known that my final position is the same I started with. . . .

Missions, my lord, missions—that is what this country needs. They will not only provide it with what is most important—the light of the Holy Gospel—but also will be the means of supplying foodstuffs for themselves and the Royal Presidios. They will accomplish this far more efficiently than these pueblos without priests. Besides, there are many other drawbacks to the plan that I might mention.

Later on, when the gentiles that are spread throughout all these lands have become Christian, and when they are settled in their various reservations or missions, in open territories or Crown lands—which will remain unsettled . . . I assure you that then will be the proper time for introducing towns of Spaniards. Let them be of good conduct and blameless life. But at present I am opposed to the plan and for many reasons.

Serra was appealing to De Croix as "the heir and of the same flesh and blood as our most excellent first founder of all this stretch of new Christianity." Yet his plea fell upon ears that had heard words of caution about the dominance of the friars. They had assumed a major role in the development of New California, and De Croix would give the order to establish pueblos as he saw fit. The next, in 1781, would bear the name of Nuestra Señora, La Reina de los Angeles del Río de Porciúncula, and give rise to the great city of Los Angeles.

The great battles between the royal prerogative and the clergy had already been fought in Spain, but they would be renewed in New California under the strong administration of Neve, backed by De Croix, and the independence and dedication of Serra. One of their bitterest struggles arose over the padre's Faculty to Confirm, usually exercised only by bishops but which in 1778 was granted to Fray Junípero because of the remoteness of this frontier.

MURDERERS FORGIVEN

Eager to spread this blessing to the neophytes at each of the missions, Serra confirmed several hundred Indians and sailors at San Carlos before he took ship for San Diego. Here he faced three of the murderers of Padre Jayme who had been shown mercy and returned to the fold. Confirming all of them, he sketched for the Viceroy a moving scene of Christian forgiveness.

> I took special care that the first to be confirmed was an Indian named Diego. At the beginning he had been faithful and a favorite of mine. But he turned traitor during the revolution and was one of the prisoners they said deserved death. I confirmed him first, then, although being sick they had to carry him into the church. Three days later he received the other Sacraments, and attended by me and also by the two other Fathers he took wings to shine in his newly won character in heaven.

After confirming six hundred at San Diego, he left there in October, traveling from mission to mission and not reaching San Carlos until the end of the year.

> On this long confirmation tour, he suffered a great deal from the habitual disease of his foot, in which he felt no improvement.
>
> [Palóu]

That fall two frigates were anchored at San Francisco after another perilous exploration that had taken them as far north as Alaska. When the ships' officers heard of the seriousness of Serra's ailment, they started to his aid with one of the royal surgeons. They revered and loved the padre, but to their surprise they encountered him at Santa Clara. In his zeal to administer confirmation, Serra had started north on foot, "casting aside all thought of his affliction and placing all his trust in God." He had walked seventy miles in two days, and could scarcely stand.

> When the officers and surgeon saw the inflammation of the leg and the wound of the foot, they declared that it was only a miracle that he could walk. The fact is that he did walk the entire journey [to San Francisco]. . . . His arrival was the occasion of extraordinary joy and festivity for all the people, both from sea and shore. . . . When they [the surgeons] sought to treat him, he put them off by saying that he felt better since he had rested. His affliction, because of its many years' duration, would undoubtedly require a longer period of treatment; and since he was remaining but a few days, it

would be useless to start it. So he said it was better to leave it in the hands of the Divine Physician.

[Palóu]

In San Francisco, he was shocked to hear news of the death of Bucareli from the same courier who brought word of the outbreak of war between Spain and England. The frigates departed immediately for San Blas. In the emergency of war, they failed to return on their regular run. Lack of supplies caused hardships in New California, where Serra was having his own tribulations with the governor. Neve had begun to challenge Serra's power to confirm, questioning whether he had sanction from the Crown as well as from Rome.

Prudently, Serra had sent the official papers back to Mexico for safe-keeping, but Neve accused him of duplicity. In defiance of him and in the humility of his faith, Serra had walked over one hundred miles to San Francisco, but Neve was exasperated. He wrote to De Croix that there was nothing that these friars "with their immeasurable and incredible pride" would not attempt. Eventually the dispute was settled in favor of Fray Junípero while Neve waited for a time when he could bring "this president to a proper acknowledgement of the authority which he eludes while pretending to obey."

"PRUDENT AS SERPENTS"

Neve had reference also to Serra's subtle opposition to the governor's move toward self-government for the Indians. Without consulting Serra, he ordered that the villages around the first five missions must annually elect their own *alcaldes* (combination of mayor and magistrate) and *regidores* (councilmen). From their close association with the natives, the padres feared chaos. They regarded the Indians as still too primitive and irresponsible to be safe from future land-grabbers without their pro-tection. The measure Neve proposed was a first step toward the seculariza-tion of the missions which, in other lands where the Indians were more familiar with the new civilization, sometimes took place in ten years.

Neve was attempting to restrict the padres only to religious matters in their authority, but he had reckoned without their rebellion. One of the ablest, Fray Fermín Francisco de Lasuén, threatened to resign his post, and he was not alone. Lasuén was stationed at San Diego, which was still struggling and impoverished, seemingly ill-starred from the first. He had remarked wryly that the reason the Indians liked him so well was doubtless because, like them, he had to dress in rags. Asking Neve for a suspension of the elections for *alcalde,* Fray Junípero had a rude encounter with him on Palm Sunday of 1779, which he described to Lasuén.

> Before Mass we exchanged a few words, and he [Neve] brought up something so flatly contrary to the truth that I was shocked, and I shouted out: "Nobody has ever said that to me because they could not say it to me!". . .
>
> He told me with irony in his voice not to worry and that the information was entirely confidential between us. . . .
>
> And so our exchange of words came to an end. That was the preparation I made for Mass on so solemn a day. I stood for a long time in front of the altar trying to calm my emotions. . . .
>
> During the rest of the day I felt wretched, being quite incapable of throwing off the obsession, and arguing with myself, in a thousand ways, as to what I should do. [He started a letter to Neve]. . . . Yet, with every sentence I wrote, something seemed to come up against it. So I stopped. I went over the matter again and again in my mind . . . and after wrestling with that letter until about midnight, to see if I could not calm myself, I took a fresh piece of paper and started to write [to one of the other friars]. . . .
>
> The thought came to me that the night was far spent, and that if I did not lie down for a while, even if I did not feel sleepy, I would be useless for anything today. . . . I got to the alcove, with the idea of finding some rest in . . . fixing my mind on some religious object. But it was all to no purpose. I just had to break out with: "What is the meaning of it all, O Lord?"
>
> And a voice within me seemed to reply in very clear words: "Be prudent as serpents and simple as doves."
>
> And I felt a new man again: "Yes, Lord, yes, Lord," I said, "thus it will be with Your grace."
>
> I fell off to sleep. At the usual time I arose to say my Office [at dawn]. . . .

And so the program I have outlined is this: whatever the gentle-man [Neve] wishes to be done should be done, but in such wise that it should not cause the least change among the Indians or disturb the routine Your Reverences have established.

What Serra counseled was that the friars see that the new offices went to certain Indians who already held some post of responsibility, such as chiefs or assistant overseers. Thus their fellow tribesmen would neither be unduly surprised nor upset.

Neve had further stipulated that the newly elected officials could not be disciplined by the padres without his consent, and the results were as they had foreseen. The *alcalde* at San Gabriel took advantage of his freedom from restraint to supply the soldiers with women, and the one at San Carlos seduced his sister-in-law and ran off to the mountains, where he induced others to join him. Insolence and insubordination undermined authority, and even Neve admitted that the *alcalde* system had serious defects.

Neve was a statesman as well as a soldier, and he was working on a document that in 1781 would give California its first complete code of legislation, the *Reglamento,* on which his fame chiefly rests. This was a form of constitution and was approved by the king. Most sweepingly it related to colonization, but the friars were profoundly disturbed by one of its concepts.

Only the stoutest spirits among them had been able to endure the exile and isolation of New California, where they lived for years on end. Now Neve was asking for more than human flesh could be expected to bear. He was recommending that, instead of two missionaries to a mission, only one be assigned. This would, he declared, reduce "the expenses of the royal treasury."

Since the padres were supported by alms from private citizens, the Pious Fund, this was scarcely a valid claim. Neve was striking at the heart of every friar already in New California or who could be expected to come to this wilderness. Even with two friars, their situation had been such that Lasuén had written: "Loneliness . . . in this work is for me a savage and cruel enemy." He described the hard-pressed life in vivid terms.

A missionary priest has to engage in many duties, many of which only concern him as means to something else. He is responsible for the spiritual and temporal welfare of people who are many and varied. He has individuals who are more dependent on him than small children, for there are many needs that arise . . . and many different things to be done for the different groups that make up the community. He is surrounded by pagans, and placed in charge of neophytes who can be trusted but little. . . .

Neve's grim proposal meant that a missionary would be forced to spend his days alone among the Indians with only one other priest fifty or sixty miles away for spiritual support and companionship. Lasuén declared that this would be "to condemn a religious to a life that is more than a burden, to sickness without attendance, and to death without the sacraments."

COLORADO MASSACRE

In the end Neve lost his case, but these were times of great trial for the missions and for Fray Junípero, who was asking, "How much longer can I last?" Under other circumstances, he would have "danced with joy," as he wrote, at news that Channel missions were finally to be established. Rivera was bringing colonists over the land route established by Anza across the Colorado River. All were unaware that the Yumas had "conceived a great hatred for the Spaniards" who had been settling in this region and depriving them of their most fertile lands where they raised squash and beans.

> So the natives decided to eject the Spaniards not only from their country, but to send them from this world by killing them and possessing themselves of their horses, of which they were very covetous. . . . Neither the soldiers nor the settlers knew anything of this plot. However . . . the missionary fathers [at the two Colorado missions] suspected something, because for a long time prior to the outbreak they began to prepare the soldiers and settlers for the acceptance of death. . . . One Sunday, after the last Mass, a great many pagans fell upon both settlements simultaneously. . . . They also killed Captain Don Fernando Rivera y Moncada and the soldiers from Monterey, all eight of whom were on the other side of the river.

[Palóu]

Few escaped, and among those massacred was the extraordinary Fray Francisco Garcés, who had been greatly loved by the Indians and who had lived much of his adventurous life alone among them. Fortunately, most of the colonists who were headed for New California and the new pueblo of Los Angeles had been sent on ahead, but the dangers of the land route had become so great that the Spaniards were forced to abandon it.

Also, Neve was forced to make a change of plan. In order to save the expense of feeding and clothing the Indians around the Channel missions, he had proposed to have them remain in their native villages instead of in a cluster of huts close to each mission, as had proved successful elsewhere in New California. Staying in their own villages made it difficult to Christianize them, and the padres deplored it. This arrangement had been tried along the Colorado, and the friars had only to point now to the bloody obliteration of all the Spaniards' plans for settlement. Opposition to Neve had reached a climax in Mexico City, where missionaries expected to head the new missions were staging what was virtually a sit-down strike.

Calamity and confusion were in the air as Fray Junípero prepared to found his last mission—San Buenaventura at the southern end of the Channel. Thirteen years had passed since he and Gálvez had first made their plans for it.

> On the last day of March [1782], the joyful Easter feast of the Resurrection, the Venerable Father President blessed the site and the holy cross. . . . The pagans of the town showed signs of joy at the arrival of their new neighbors, and willingly aided in setting up the chapel.
>
> [Palóu]

FAGES RETURNS

In this same year Neve was elevated to the inspector-generalship of all the troops of the Interior Provinces, and Fages took his place as governor of the Californias. Don Pedro had matured with experience, and he was soon to be joined by his wife, Doña Eulalia. She was the first woman of quality to travel to New California and a spirited mate. Quarrels with her husband coupled with her generosity to the Indians added color to the gray monotony of Monterey.

1782

Hubert A. Lowman, courtesy California Mission Trails Association, Ltd.

Mission San Buenaventura.

Fages had stated upon his return that he wished to be a friend of the padres and aid them in their efforts but had to act under Neve's control. Frictions lessened, and a few years later he paid high tribute to the accomplishments of the missions under Fray Junípero in the conquest of California. He had witnessed them from their very beginnings, and during Serra's lifetime they had converted some five thousand Indians. Though there were rumors that the Dominicans might take them over, they continued under the Franciscan order.

> It is they [the Franciscans] who commenced the grand work amid the poverty, penury, and want which are inseparable from such undertakings in newly discovered countries. Here the difficulties were aggravated on account of the immense distance from every civilized land. Nevertheless, these religious have placed their institutions on a solid basis. If we must do justice to all, as is obligatory, we must confess that the rapid, agreeable, and interesting progress in spiritual as well as temporal affairs which we happily observe and enjoy is the glorious effect of the apostolic zeal, activity, and indefatigable efforts of these religious.
>
> [Fages]

Serra did not live to hear of this report to the superior government. He had a serious chest condition and could scarcely draw breath, but he was determined to pay a final visit to all the missions. Scarcely in fit condition to sail to San Diego and make the return journey by land, he departed in August of 1783, writing a farewell note to Palóu, who was to be his successor.

> He concluded by saying with much grace and resignation: "I say all this because my return may be only a death warrant, so seriously ill do I feel. Commend me to God." Despite the fact that he felt so ill, the zealous and fervent fire in his heart made him put off all thought of his own health and life in favor of his love for his neighbors, since he would not deprive them of the spiritual benefits of the holy sacrament of Confirmation. [The faculty would expire in the following year.]
>
> [Palóu]

A man of peace, Fray Junípero had known long turbulence, but the mission walls would not crumble for many years. Defending them and their growth with his deep faith and his fortitude, he had been able to see them through their most vulnerable period. He gave heart to missionaries who could see no future here with a parable that could have applied to himself.

> One of our communities of religious had just started Matins, and before long a friar went up to the Guardian and whispered: "Father, may I retire to my cell? I am not feeling well."
>
> The Superior's answer was: "Brother, for the love of God, stay in your place. I can assure you that if all the choir who are not feeling well were to leave, there would be no Matins. All of us, and I first of all, would leave."
>
> [Serra]

SOARING SPIRIT

Serra was a heroic figure in Spain's last great conquest, refusing to admit defeat in the face of starvation, death, and official obstacles. True, he had his enemies and his human faults. The military commanders often accused him of being single-minded; his thirst for converting souls was never quenched. And yet here was a man who had left his cloister and his books to step out into life with its anxieties, frustrations, angers, and joys to use all of himself.

His was a triumph of the human spirit over odds that would have overwhelmed any but a great and remarkable man and missionary, and thus he has gone down in the history of California and of the United States. He was the man who always went forward and never turned back even when, as at San Diego, brave explorers were ready to abandon New California to the sea gulls, the antelopes, and the Indians.

During this seventieth year of his life, he made his slow and painful way between the missions, covering over five hundred miles, to the astonishment of his colleagues, who never expected to see him alive. In August of 1784, he sent a call to Palóu, who arrived at San Carlos to find him reciting the catechism, as usual, with the neophytes.

When I heard him sing with his voice as strong as usual, I remarked to a soldier who was talking to me: "It does not seem that the Father President is very sick." The soldier, who had known him since 1769, answered me: "Father, there is no basis for hope: he is ill. This saintly priest is always well when it comes to praying or singing, but he is nearly finished."

One of Serra's last acts as he prepared for death was to cut up cloth that had come by one of the ships and distribute it among the neophytes, and to give an old Indian woman half of the blanket that covered his bed of boards. The ship's surgeon tried to treat the congestion in his chest, but Serra got his only relief leaning against the bed or against the arms of the devoted Indians who crowded into his cell. Having received the last rites of the church, his end was peaceful, and he was "now asleep in the Lord." The date was August 28, 1784.

> As soon as the double peal [of the bells] rang out the sad news, the whole town assembled, weeping over the death of their beloved father. . . . So great was the crowd of people, including Indians and soldiers and sailors, that it was necessary to close the door. . . . Every half hour [on the following day of the funeral] a cannon was fired, which was answered by another volley from the presidio. . . These intermittent salutes, with the mournful tolling of the bells, melted the hearts of all.
>
> [Palóu]

Fray Junípero was laid to rest beside Padre Crespí, who had died two years previously, and it was, as Palóu wrote, "as if some general was being buried."

GRAVE of
FATHER
SERRA

Serra's grave under the altar floor of Mission San Carlos de Monterey, Carmel.

WHAT HAPPENED AFTERWARD

During the year following Serra's death, Palóu took his place as president of the missions, putting aside his notes for a valuable first history, *Historical Memoirs of New California,* to work on the life story of his closest friend. He had long wished to retire to Mexico; after a year, he relinquished the office to Fray Fermín Francisco de Lasuén, under whom the missions reached their golden age. Padre Serra had laid their foundations and fought their first battles.

Stone by stone and adobe brick by brick, the missions were built around their central plazas to replace the early log structures with architecture that had the beauty of simplicity. Skilled artisans came from Mexico to guide the labor of the neophytes. Pomegranates grew crimson against the arches of the colonnades; orange and lemon trees shaded the thick outer walls; gates gave glimpses of rose gardens; swallows nested under the eaves.

Increasing travelers along *El Camino Real* found food and rest at the chain of twenty-one missions that eventually stretched from south to north in oases of peace and beauty. As Padre Serra had desired, the Indians decorated the whitewashed walls of the churches brilliantly with direct expressions of their art. Flowers, angels, and suns made a setting for the carved wooden images and the elaborate silver vessels and candlesticks brought up from Mexico, mingling the reverence of two cultures. Symbolically, many of the outer doors bore the curved pattern of the River of Life.

Under Lasuén, as under Serra, kindness and patience were the general rule, and neophytes were punished much as unruly children might be disciplined by their fathers. Charges that the padres kept the Indians under lock and key were true only of the unmarried maidens, and the neophytes often were permitted to go back to their old lives for several weeks, returning frequently with some of their relatives. They were treated far more harshly at the presidios.

The padres tried to be physicians of the body as well as the soul, but still the converted Indians had a high death rate. Though they were fed better at the missions and were protected from warring tribes, they were crowded into *rancherías* where the white man's diseases could spread. They had little resistance to new infections. Also, when they came to live at the missions, they more or less ceased their old practice of burning down their houses occasionally as a native measure of sanitation. Further, the Indian men seldom made use of the sweat houses that they had once used to treat the sick.

Other aspects of these religious communities, besides the high death toll, were criticized by the first foreigner permitted to land on the shores of New California. He was the distinguished French navigator Count Jean François de la Pérouse, who stopped at Monterey for ten days in the fall of 1786, bound for his ill-fated scientific voyage of exploration around the world. La Pérouse saw in the missions a veritable theocracy under which the neophytes believed that the friars were "in immediate and direct communication with God."

Imbued with the ideas of freedom and liberty that were soon to lead to the French Revolution, he felt that the Indians were treated too much like children and too little like men. He deplored the fact that soldiers were sent to bring back converts who had run away to the mountains and, like Neve, thought they should have more civil liberties.

In his opinion, civilizing them would be furthered if a few families at least might be given property rights, a beginning that might show others the advantage of cultivating their own fields. However, he admitted that progress under this new plan would be slow and that it would be attended with such difficulties that earthly human motives could not suffice. La Pérouse recognized that only the zeal of religion and its promise of rewards in heaven enabled the padres to endure the fatigues and dangers of their lonely lives. Though he was critical of their austerity, he admired their character. Of Lasuén he wrote: "His mildness, charity, and affection for the Indians are beyond expression."

Two to three thousand head of cattle were slaughtered each year at the most populous missions to supply the neophytes. The Indians had their three meals a day at the missions, in addition to the native foods which they gathered themselves, such as game, acorns, and shellfish. As one of the padres noted, "On account of this hodgepodge of eatables, which they have in their homes and to their being like children who eat at all hours, it is hard to determine how much they eat every day."

After 1821, when Mexico won its independence from Spain, the missions steadily declined in popularity. The Church had opposed independence, and settlers were covetous of lands that supported a rich and abundant agriculture. The padres had chosen sagely and improved them with irrigation, so that they controlled some of the choicest acreage in the whole province.

Freedom for the Indians became the cry, and constant accusations were made that the padres enslaved them. In 1833, the Mexican Congress passed

Reception of La Pérouse at Mission San Carlos de Monterey in 1786.

Marie Van Auken, courtesy Carme

Reçivimiento del Conde delas Fri Rues enla mission del Carmelo de Mon a bill to secularize all the missions of California, changing their role to that of parish churches. They were stripped of lands and livestock that presumably were to go half to the Indians and half into the hands of government administrators. Deprived of the protection of the friars, the Indians were shortly defrauded as greedy politicans and ranchers shared the spoils. They lingered about the missions which had been their homes but which were no longer able to support them. With civilization, they had lost their original independence and were bewildered to be thrown again upon their own resources. Whites proceeded to take over camp sites where the hunting was good and, with the discovery of gold, to destroy the food sources of streams with their mining operations. The Indians became a pathetic remnant of their former numbers, dwindling to around sixteen thousand by the beginning of the twentieth century.

After secularization, few of the missions were able to survive as parish churches. They were looted and abandoned to fall into ruins. Shaken by the earthquakes of land and of history, they vanished for many years into the past. Roofs fell in . . . adobe walls melted with the winter rains . . . lizards skittered over the stones.

Today all of them have been restored, at least in part. A few are museums only, but most are the center of active parishes. Several are also Franciscan monasteries; one is a college, another a university. As the modern traveler sits among the flowers and fountains of these mission gardens, shielded from the outside world by high walls, he can perhaps see the shadow of a leather-jacket soldier . . . of Indian children playing in the dust . . . of Fray Junípero riding into the plaza on muleback to the joyful tolling of the bells.

DRAMATIS PERSONAE

Many played important roles in this drama of history:

JUAN BAUTISTA DE ANZA, frontier fighter, explorer, and skillful colony leader who opened the land route from the mainland of Mexico. He safely conducted a large party of men, women, and children some sixteen hundred miles to New California, not losing a single life. It was a record seldom equaled in any pioneer trek.

MIGUEL COSTANSÓ, army engineer and cosmographer of the original expedition sent to settle New California. An intelligent and acute observer, he wrote vividly of the hazards and hardships.

FRAY JUAN CRESPÍ, student of Serra's in Palma who came with him to Mexico in 1749. He accompanied the first land expedition to New California, was one of the discoverers of San Francisco Bay, and sailed as far north as Canada. A notable missionary, explorer and diarist, he resided at the San Carlos mission with Serra almost from its founding until his death twelve years later.

ANTONIO MARÍA BUCARELI Y URSUA, Viceroy of New Spain who worked with Serra to relieve the distress of the missions at their most crucial stage. After Serra's trip to Mexico City to see him, this Spanish aristocrat became a strong supporter and admirer, and proved to be the best friend the missions ever had.

CARLOS FRANCISCO DE CROIX, Viceroy of New Spain who initiated the sea and land move into New California. He held Serra in great esteem and praised his zeal and dedication.

TEODORO DE CROIX, nephew of Carlos, who did not inherit his uncle's enthusiasm for the work of the missions when he took over their jurisdiction from Bucareli. He had been cautioned not to let the friars become too dominant, and during Serra's later years raised many obstructions.

JUAN EVANGELISTA, converted Indian boy who accompanied Serra to Mexico City and returned to tell his people of the wonders of civilization.

EULALIA CALLIS FAGES, spirited wife of Don Pedro Fages, who was the first woman of quality to come to New California.

PEDRO FAGES, first military commandant at Monterey, who later returned as governor. During this first period, he was young, inexperienced, and meddlesome, though efficient. This brought him into serious conflict with Padre Serra and threatened the whole conquest. By the time he was governor in Serra's last years, he had matured and later paid high tribute to the work of the missionaries.

FRAY PEDRO FONT, missionary and diarist, who accompanied Anza and the colonists from Mexico and left graphic accounts of life at the missions and on the trail.

JOSÉ DE GÁLVEZ, Inspector-General and activator of the occupation of New California. He had an intensity and drive to match Serra's, and together they made an extraordinary team. Later he became Minister of the Indies.

FRAY FRANCISCO TOMÁS GARCÉS, adventurous missionary who traveled extensively alone among the Indians exploring unknown territory and acted as a guide for Anza. Slain in the Yuma massacre along the Colorado.

FRAY LUIS JAYME, California's first martyr, who lost his life in the Indian attack on San Diego.

FRAY FERMÍN FRANCISCO DE LASUÉN, successor to Serra who raised the New California missions to their peak of prosperity and was known for his graciousness, sweetness of temper, and devotion to the Indians, as well as for his diplomatic skill. He was a highly intelligent Basque, and only thirty-seven when he first came to the province.

FELIPE DE NEVE, soldier and statesman who, as governor, gave California its first complete code of legislation but endeavored to block the work of the friars in the development of the province. He and Serra had many bitter battles, since Neve had strong political influence in Mexico and Spain.

JOSÉ FRANCISCO ORTEGA, courageous chief scout for Portolá and favored by Serra to replace Fages. He was then only a sergeant and considered by Bucareli to be of too low rank for the post of commandant.

FRAY FRANCISCO PALÓU, Serra's closest friend and a student of his at Palma. Palóu accompanied Serra to Mexico, served with him in the Sierra Gorda, founded the mission at San Francisco, and temporarily became his successor. Devoted and able, he wrote a valuable first history of California and a life of Serra which have been major sources for all future historians.

JUAN PÉREZ, sea captain and expert navigator who participated in the initial conquest of New California and later explored the coast as far north as Canada. Like Serra, he came from Palma, and the two were good friends.

GASPAR DE PORTOLÁ, governor of the two Californias who commanded the first expedition to San Diego with Serra, missed Monterey, and discovered San Francisco Bay. He was liked by both soldiers and padres, and later became governor of Pueblo, New Spain.

PEDRO PRAT, surgeon on the first expedition to New California. He went insane within a few years.

FERNANDO DE RIVERA Y MONCADA, leader of the first land expedition to New California in 1769 who succeeded Fages as military commander of the province. He was popular with his soldiers but vacillating and timid, to the frustration of Padre Serra. Later he became lieutenant-governor of Old California and was killed by the Yumas in the massacre along the Colorado.

FRAY RAFAEL VERGER, professorial colleague of Serra's in Palma who accompanied him to Mexico and became Guardian of the College of San Fernando. He often thought Serra overzealous and advised caution. He was later named Bishop of Nueva Leon.

VICENTE VILA, captain of the *San Carlos,* on which Serra resolved to remain if Portolá abandoned San Diego.

BABBLE OF TONGUES

Because of the great variety of Indian dialects, to the number of about a hundred and thirty-five, it was difficult to transfer the padres from one mission to another. Efforts were made to teach the Indians to speak Castilian, but it was chiefly children who became the linguists. The following words were taken from that spoken by the Indians along the Santa Barbara Channel which the Spaniards found to be sonorous and easy to pronounce.

Words in that language.	Their equivalent in Spanish.	
Nucchú	La Cabeza	head
Kejuhé	El Pecho	breast
Huachajá	La Mano	hand
Chipucú	El Codo	elbow
Tocholó	El Sobaco	armpit
Tononomó	El Muslo	thigh
Pistocú	La Rodilla	knee
Kippejué	La Pierna	leg
Acteme	El Pie	foot
Tomol	Lancha o Canoa	canoe
Apa	Ranchería	village
Temi	Capitán o Principal	chief
Amo	No	no

	Numerals.	
Pacá	Uno	one
Excó	Dos	two
Maseja	Tres	three
Scumu	Cuatro	four

Itipaca	Cinco	five
Itixco	Seis	six
Itismasge	Siete	seven
Malahua	Ocho	eight
Upax	Nueve	nine
Kerxco	Diez	ten

The many regional dialects were associated with the territories occupied by the various Indian communities, so loosely knit that it has been said they scarcely could be called tribes in the usual sense. Each had marked out its own boundaries, and invasion of them by other natives often led to bloody fights.

CALIFORNIA'S MISSION CHAIN

Twenty-one missions offered hospitality to travelers north and south along *El Camino Real* over a stretch of more than five hundred miles. The first nine were founded by Fray Junípero himself or during his time, and the next nine under Lasuén. All of them have been restored, at least in part.

SAN DIEGO DE ALCALÁ   July 16, 1769

SAN CARLOS DE MONTEREY   June 3, 1770

SAN ANTONIO DE PADUA   July 14, 1771

SAN GABRIEL DE LOS TEMBLORES   September 8, 1771

SAN LUIS OBISPO DE TOLOSA   September 1, 1772

SAN FRANCISCO DE ASÍS   October 9, 1776

SAN JUAN CAPISTRANO   November 1, 1776

SANTA CLARA DE ASÍS   January 12, 1777

SAN BUENAVENTURA   March 31, 1782

SANTA BÁRBARA   December 4, 1786

LA PURÍSIMA CONCEPCIÓN   December 8, 1787

SANTA CRUZ   August 28, 1791

NUESTRA SEÑORA DE LA SOLEDAD   October 9, 1791

SAN JOSÉ DE GUADALUPE   June 11, 1797

SAN JUAN BAUTISTA   June 24, 1797

SAN MIGUEL ARCÁNGEL   July 25, 1797

SAN FERNANDO REY DE ESPAÑA   September 8, 1797

SAN LUIS REY DE FRANCIA   June 13, 1798

SANTA INÉS   September 17, 1804

SAN RAFAEL ARCÁNGEL   December 14, 1817

SAN FRANCISCO DE SOLANO   July 4, 1823

ADORNING THE WILDERNESS

Though the padres themselves might be living in miserable huts, the House of the Lord must have furnishings fit for a cathedral. After San Diego was plundered and burned, Serra sent to Bucareli this typical list of church needs to make it possible to appeal to the Indians with spiritual and beautiful ceremony.

One white chasuble, with stole, maniple, chalice veil, etc.

Item another red, with the same accessories.

Item another purple, with the same accessories.

Item another green, with the said additions.

Item another black, with the said additions.

Item another five antependiums of the same colors and materials as the said five chasubles.

Item five tabernacle veils of the same five colors with their accessories.

Item three copes, i. e., one white, one purple, one black corresponding to the three chasubles of a like color.

Item one mozzetta, or cope, with a stole to correspond, for the administration of the Holy Viaticum.

Item a canopy furnished with poles, or without them, for the administration of the same Holy Sacrament.

Item a white *dalmaisal* for the same purpose.

Item a white banner for the same purpose with the insignia of the Blessed Sacrament on one side and of San Diego on the other, with streamers attached.

Item thirteen silver coins and six rings of the same metal and a purse to hold them, which are the *arras* for marriage rites.

Item two caps made of Brittany linen, trimmed with lace and ribbons; a large one for the Baptisms of adults, the other small for children.

Item a set of altar cards: a middle altar card, the Gospel of Saint John, and a Lavabo card.

Item four or six large candlesticks three-fourths of a vara high for the altar.

Item in reference to the sacred vessels of silver, that is, the chalice, ciborium, oil stocks, cruets, small plate, altar bell, saltcellar, baptism shell, censer, etc., which, having had them melted down by fire, I forwarded them to our College to have them made over. I request that the cost for the work be paid if some benefactor has not paid for it already.

Item a blue and red shag carpet, three varas long and two wide, lined with cotton, for the foot of the altar.

Item another carpet of the same quality but smaller, two varas long and one wide, for the small altar in the house of the sick, used whenever the Most Holy Viaticum is administered.

Item a small white antependium decorated with flowers, one vara long by a half wide or a little larger for the said small altar.

Item a sacrarium conforming to the rubrics with its linen and little cup of gilded glass, made in such size that it can be easily taken away and carried from place to place.

Item a trunk of cedarwood, wide and not very high in which the said vestments—carefully wrapped—will come. Let the chest have lock and key. This will be very useful in the said mission, to keep them in, seeing that there is a great scarcity of timber there suitable for making one.

FOR THE RECORD

The padres at the various missions kept careful accounts to be sent each year to the superior government and to justify the expense to the Crown. Eventually the missions were expected to become self-sustaining. This is Serra's report for 1774.

Name of the missions:	San Diego de Alcalá	San Gabriel de los Temblores	San Luis Obispo	San Antonio de Padua	San Carlos de Monterey	Total
Founded:	July 16, 1769	Sept. 8, 1771	Sept. 1, 1772	July 14, 1771	June 3, 1770	
Baptisms:	116	148	108	194	267	833
Marriages:	19	19	28	22	36	124
Deceased:	19	8	5	19	23	74
Living:	97	140	103	175	244	759
Cows:	54	65	65	59	61	304
Sheep:	104	66	0	0	0	170
Goats:	61	34	0	0	0	95
Pigs:	27	18	13	40	32	130
Mares:	15	4	3	5	4	31
Colts:	11	8	3	5	3	30
Tame horses:	9	7	9	7	17	39
Mules:	22	16	18	15	14	85
Donkeys:	3	0	0	0	1	4
Wheat, Sown:	7 fs.	6 fs.	4 fs.	2 fs.	3½ fs.	22½ fs.
Harvested:	30 fs.	90 fs.	200 fs.	30 fs.	125 fs.	475 fs.
Corn, Sown:	0	13 alms.	3 alms.	7 alms.	8 alms.	4 f. 7 alms.
Harvested:	0	240 fs.	80 fs.	70 fs.	150 fs.	540 fs.
Beans, Planted:	0	7 alms.	½ alms.	0	6 alms.	13½ alms.
Harvested:	0	30 fs.	3 fs.	0	7 fs.	40 fs.

Note: A *fanega* (pl. *fs.*) was 1.6 bushels; an *almud* (pl. *alms.*) was a measure varying from 2 to 21 quarts.

MISSION HOUSEKEEPING

Hundreds of articles were required to set up a mission, and in the early days all of them had to be transported from Mexico. Any homely item forgotten might take years to replace, and Fray Junípero was meticulous in his preparation of this list for an unnamed mission sent to Bucareli in 1775. Rosaries "with good and durable wiring" . . . "a thousand tacks with large heads"—the variety and scope help picture life on this remote frontier and the problems the padres faced—particularly when supplies failed to arrive.

First, a devotional Crucifix of what we call hand-size, or for the pulpit—the principal object of our preaching—for the altar.

Item, a painting of the Patron or Titular Saint of the mission: the size a vara and half in height, and of a corresponding width, with a gilded frame; let the frame come in separate pieces and let there be a reinforcing middle stick. Let it be by a good painter.

Six small copper pots, soldered, or divers sizes for the kitchen and for other uses, as for instance for washing, etc.
Six frying pans of the same material and soldered.
Six flat-iron pans with their handles, for the same purpose.
Six copper soldered pots of different sizes and shapes with their covers, and let one of them be very large.
A large pail, or a large pozole pot for meals for the Indians.
Two large dippers in the shape of half an orange.
A box of beads and some trinkets, such as combs, scissors, etc.
Some papers of shoemakers' needles to be used by the Indian women.

A gross of small crosses, of metal, of the small size.

Another gross of larger crosses of the same kind.

Two gross of medals, of different sizes.

Twelve gross of rosaries; let the wiring be good and durable.

Six carpenter axes and twelve axes suitable for chopping wood to make charcoal.

Two dozen hoes.

Two double-handed adzes, and six machetes.

Two hand adzes.

Four bits of different sizes and steeled.

Five Castilian plowshares (shod).

Six corn grinders with their pestles.

Four small metal candlesticks with extinguishers.

Two sets of inkwells with sand boxes of bronze or lead.

Six untrimmed Mexican skins.

Two dozen raw cowhides for yoke thongs.

Two dozen leather bags.

Twelve sets of leather harness with all their accessories, straps, buckles, etc.

Two outfits for the equipment of a packtrain.

Six skeins of thread for sewing leather.

Twelve pounds of loose thread.

A dozen pack needles.

Six skeins of packthread.

Two cowboy's saddles with their accessories.

Two riding saddles for the trips and journeyings of the Fathers.

Four bridles with their trimmings, etc.

Six blank record books bound in sheepskin, for baptism records, burials, marriages, inventories, etc.

One arroba of Castillian wax for Mass purposes.

Wine for Mass purposes.

A bottle case to keep it under key.

Six locks for cases with corresponding hinges or hooks.

Two large bolts with their fastenings, one for the church and the other for the granary.

Six door locks and two dozen hinges.

A dozen plates, and another of cups of china, metal, or some such material.

Two pitchers for drinking water, of metal or soldered copper.

Two wire strainers to strain corn flour.

Four strainers with their hoops, two for rough usage, the other two for finer work.

Two iron spoons, and a skimmer of the same metal.

A dozen small horn spoons for the table.

A case of shaving knives with strop and whetstone.

A small tin cup for shaving.

Some balance scales with its weight of eighteen pounds.

A Roman scale with its ball or weight.

A jointing plane, jack plane, plane, and carpenter's hammer.

A drop-hammer, hammer, stove pick, trowel, and mason's plumb; let it be a whole double set.

Two dozen large knives, and one of small knives.

A gross of nails a quarter of a vara long.

A gross of brace nails.

Another gross of half-brace nails.

Another gross of nails from Tajamanil.

A thousand tacks with large heads.

Six drills of divers sizes.

Two chisels.

To be able to make a start in clothing the naked: Six bolts of coarse cotton cloth.

Three bolts of striped coarse woolen cloth.

One bolt of baize or thick flannel, and a half-bolt of Querétaro cloth, for the Indians from California who will act as servants.

A hundred sheepherders' blankets for all.

BIBLIOGRAPHY

Anza's California Expeditions. 2 vols. Translated from the original Spanish and edited by Herbert Eugene Bolton. University of California Press. Berkeley, 1930.

Bancroft, Hubert Howe: *History of California,* vol. 1 (1542–1800). Bancroft, San Francisco, 1884

Bolton, Herbert E.: *Fray Juan Crespí.* University of California Press. Berkeley, 1927.

Bolton, Herbert E.: *The Mission as a Frontier Institution in the Spanish-American Colonies.* American Historical Review, vol. 23, October 1917. Macmillan, London, 1918

Chapman, Charles E.: *Founding of Spanish California.* Macmillan, New York, 1916

Costansó, Miguel: *Diary.* The Portolá Expedition of 1769–70. Edited by Frederick J. Teggart. Academy of Pacific Coast History. University of California, Berkeley, August 1911

Costansó, Miguel: *Narrative of the Portolá Expedition 1769–70.* Edited by Adolph von Hemert-Engert and Frederick J. Teggart. Academy of Pacific Coast History. University of California, Berkeley, March 1910

Fages, Pedro: *A Historical, Political and Natural Description of California.* Translated by Herbert Ingram Priestley. University of California Press. Berkeley, 1937

Font, Pedro: *Diary.* The Anza Expedition of 1775–6. Academy of Pacific Coast History. University of California. Berkeley, March 1913

Geiger, Maynard J.: *Life and Times of Fray Junípero Serra O.F.M.* 2 vols. Academy of American Franciscan History. Washington, 1959

Hittell, Theodore H.: *History of California.* vol. 1. Stone, San Francisco, 1897

Lasuén, Fermín Francisco de: *Writings.* 2 vols. Academy of American Franciscan History, Washington, 1965

Maynard, Theodore: *The Long Road of Father Serra.* Appleton, New York, 1954

Palóu, Francisco: *Historical Memoirs of New California.* 4 vols. Edited by Herbert Eugene Bolton. University of California Press. Berkeley, 1926

Palóu, Francisco: *Life of Fray Junípero Serra.* Translated and annotated by Maynard J. Geiger, O.F.M., Ph.D. Academy of American Franciscan History. Washington, 1955

Portolá, Gaspar de: *Diary during the California Expedition of 1769-70.* Edited by Donald Eugene Smith and Frederick J. Teggart. Academy of Pacific Coast History. University of California, Berkeley, October 1909

Priestley, Herbert I.: *José de Gálvez.* University of California Press, Berkeley, 1916

Rolle, Andrew: *California, a History.* Crowell, New York, 1963

Serra, Junípero: *Writings.* Edited by Antonine Tibesar O.F.M. 3 vols. Academy of American Franciscan History. Washington, 1955

Webb, Edith: *Indian Life at the Old Missions.* Lewis, Los Angeles, 1952

INDEX